Albert **Speer** in the Federal Republic
Dealing with the German Past

Exhibition Catalogue
Documentation Centre Party Rally Grounds
for Nuremberg Municipal Museums
Editors: Martina Christmeier and Alexander Schmidt

Publication Series by Nuremberg Municipal Museums
Volume 13
Edited by Ingrid Bierer

Contributions by Magnus Brechtken,
Martina Christmeier, Florian Dierl,
Hanne Leßau and Alexander Schmidt

The exhibition was developed in
cooperation with the
Institute for Contemporary History
in Munich – Berlin

The catalogue was sponsored by

STIFTUNG
MERCATOR

**Nuremberg
Municipal Museums
Documentation Centre
Party Rally Grounds**

Contents

Introduction

Albert Speer is probably the most quoted eye witness of the 20th century. A committed National Socialist, Hitler's accomplice, architect-manager, war logistician, armament organiser, co-promoter of Nazi racial policies, a central figure of the war of aggression and extermination – that was the real Speer until 1945.

His image from the post-war years hardly corresponded to this. Then, Speer was usually depicted as a member of the bourgeoisie led astray by the Nazis, an apolitical technocrat, an industrious expert, who focused mainly on his work, and who maintained that he was hardly aware of any of the crimes which happened while he made pacts with the SS, drove slave labourers into misery and death and managed the war industry all over Europe. He claimed that at most he had some dark forebodings of what was happening right in front of his eyes, and what had been directly initiated by him.

This was the legend of the uninvolved, almost clueless German citizen Albert Speer firmly on the guilt-free side of German history. On the other side, there were the uncouth Nazi party men with their loud-mouthed behaviour, and their coarse mugs. These were "the Nazis", not him. Somehow he had become close to them. Why, one wonders? Naïve historians then talked about the "Speer mystery" and avoided taking a closer look at the resources.

In fact, between 1933 and 1945, nobody demanded that Speer committed himself to Hitler and National Socialism. He acted on his own free will, driven by ambition. The question "Who is a National Socialist?" must be answered with: Anybody acting in a National Socialist manner is a Nazi. And that is what Speer did after joining the Nazi party in 1931.

Albert Speer at the *3rd Reich Roll-call of the Working Youth*, on 17 October, 1943 (ullstein bild 00055227)

Albert Speer meeting journalists after his release from prison, on 1 October, 1966 (sz-photo 602137)

Every single step of his commitment was ambitious and eager, against the German Jews and other minorities, later on for the war and the enslavement of millions of workers. Speer wanted to act like this; this career was his life's work.

After 1945, Speer constructed stories distancing himself from all this, fables about personal alienation and remorse. He posed as the supposed honest confessor, in order to account for himself to posterity. With his remembrance texts, he succeeded in building a second career after 1966. As a "noble Nazi with guaranteed remorse" he was internationally in demand, became the chief witness for the alleged authenticity of evil overcome. Millions of Germans were happy to hear and read this. They almost seemed to long for these forever new and yet forever similar reports of insight and reformation. In other countries, too, hundreds of thousands demanded to see the distinguished-looking elderly gentleman with the reserved demeanour. Particularly in the Anglo-Saxon world, Speer, after his release from prison, was a welcome visitor, almost paid court to, a guest of newspapers, films and TV.

What seems to be two lives, before and after 1945, perpetrator here, remorse and skilful dissociation on the other hand, on closer inspection turns out to be a consistent story. After his time as Nazi perpetrator, Speer wanted to gain the prerogative of interpretation so that he could retell almost everything he had done, cover it with a smoke screen, and dissolve it with distracting words. Both as a perpetrator and as a re-teller, Speer was as energetic as successful. This, too, makes his career an exemplary one.

If you focus on Nazi rule as a whole and rid yourself of the erroneous idea that "the Nazis" were something alien which overwhelmed society from the outside in 1933 and disappeared as aliens in 1945, it becomes clear: Albert Speer was one of millions of Germans, namely the functional elites, who acted as National Socialists, who aligned their lives and their careers with the success of the regime. They wanted Hitler in power and with him themselves. Speer's career was outstanding, but its core was also a mirror image of the careers of many people with similar ambitions who committed themselves to National Socialism, supported it and shaped it.

A look at history textbooks and films will maybe lead to amazement, maybe to frustration: a substantial part of everything produced about the Third Reich over decades has been infiltrated with Speer's fables. For much too long, Speer's ubiquitous presence as an eye witness also exploited the work of historians and publicists and misled people. It is high time to juxtapose the legends with the enlightenment of contemporary resources. This deconstruction also mirrors a change in German society. A change from an audience who wanted to believe Speer, almost blindly, in order to exonerate themselves, to a civil society which weighs all available information in a sober and fact-based manner. To understand the past you need the will to inform yourself and to think for yourself. For this purpose, the Documentation Centre Party Rally Grounds and the Institute for Contemporary History have cooperated to make information and knowledge available, so that you can form and develop your own opinions.

Magnus Brechtken
Deputy Director
Institute for Contemporary History
Munich-Berlin

Editorial

When on 1 October, 1966, precisely at midnight, the prison gates in Berlin-Spandau opened, more than a thousand curious onlookers waited for Albert Speer and Baldur von Schirach who had completed their 20-year prison sentences. Microphones and cameras from all over the world were mainly directed at Speer who from then on was to enjoy the limelight for many years. During National Socialism, Albert Speer had been the Reich's first architect, responsible for major projects such as the Party Rally Grounds in Nuremberg and the redesign of Berlin. Almost immediately, he became one of Hitler's closest confidants. In 1942, he was appointed Minister of Armament. In 1946, the Allied Powers, in the Nuremberg Trial of the Main War Criminals sentenced him to 20 years' imprisonment.

After his release from prison in 1966, Speer's third career as a feted and seemingly reformed eye witness and author began. Through numerous TV interviews, innumerable articles in magazines and book publications, Speer was able to broadcast his legend to the public, a legend first created in 1945 in Nuremberg and then formulated in more and more detail.

He – and with him also most Germans – had not known about the crimes of National Socialism and had become involved in the war through no fault of his own, led astray by Hitler's aura. Most of all, he had not had any knowledge of the systematic murder of European Jews.

In contrast to his own depiction, Speer was far from being just Hitler's architect and later on the apolitical technocrat heading the Armament Ministry. Documents prove that rather he was one of the main perpetrators of the National Socialist regime and made significant contributions to the persecution of the Jews and to the crimes in the concentration camps.

The exhibition in the Documentation Centre set itself the task of making visible the Speer legend of the seduced, clueless technocrat and thus also the way Germans dealt with their past, in an almost forensic manner. In the Documentation Centre's large Exhibition Hall, based on the current state of research – in the past two years alone, several dissertations and articles have been published on this topic – it shows how for decades Speer, as a much-in-demand eye witness, was able to cover up historical facts with his stories. Parallel to this, there is the question of why this legend met with so much resonance in the Federal Republic for such a long time and with so many people – even after historians had long refuted many of these stories with facts from the archives.

Visitors to the exhibition will find out how Speer succeeded in creating a kind of reaffirming cycle for his fables with the continuous repetition of his "life audio tape" in the media and his alleged authenticity as an eye witness. First of all, Speer himself will have his say, with numerous examples from magazines, newspapers, and TV. Visitors can also see the uncritical alacrity with which historians and publicists, but also the German population gratefully followed the manipulative memories of the "good Nazi" – not least, because Speer had social support from a bourgeois network and provided a most welcome alibi for the many who claimed to have known nothing, but who themselves had offered their services to National Socialism.

In the third part of the exhibition, statements by experts and resources from archives prove Speer's leading involvement in Nazi crimes, allowing visitors to appreciate Speer's claims in their historical context and correct his image.

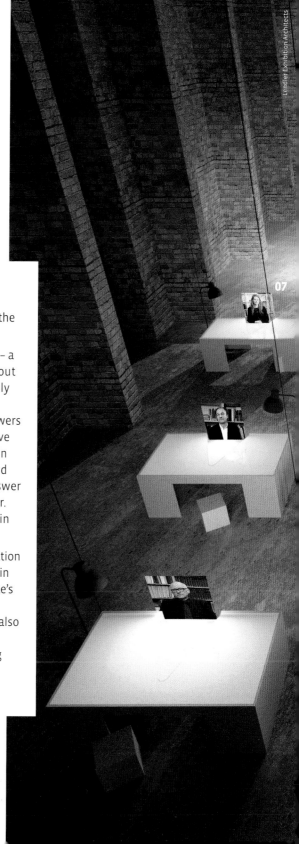

07

Speer without SPEER
Scenography and Content of the Exhibition

Exhibitions present history in space – and the unfinished Congress Hall provides sufficient space for this purpose. At 40 metres' long, eleven metres' high and eleven metres' wide, the large Exhibition Hall is a meaningful relic of the thinking of the Nazi time. The exhibition does not intend to stage Speer, but by presenting historical facts aims to refute his self-staging. Nevertheless (as was the case for decades in the post-war history of the Federal Republic) there is first of all no way around the "Speer brand". Visitors will be faced with an installation of the letters of his surname, as they marked the titles of all his books: SPEER – the logo of the Speer brand. Here, you are exposed to Speer's "life audio tape", you see and hear his for ever repeated justifications, and you sense that all of this can't be true: "I knew nothing of those horrible things."

After leaving the installation, you can still hear Speer's statements – as a background noise – but you cannot and must not listen to him any longer, but turn to historical facts. An analysis of the birth of the Speer legend before and during the Nuremberg Trial, the fixation on Hitler as the only person responsible for the crimes of National Socialism, as well as the decades of disregard for the voices of victims, together form a

pattern to explain Speer's success. This also includes his networks before and after 1945, as well as his systematic self-publicity from the 1930s right through until his death in 1981.

Many allegedly "unanswerable questions" – a book title by Joachim C. Fest with notes about his conversations with Speer – can definitely be answered, if you consult resources in archives and not only Speer's tales. The answers will be provided by nine historians who have presented studies concerning Speer's role in National Socialism in the past few years and decades. As "waiting experts", they will answer the questions Speer did not want to answer. Resources which are shown on their desks in the exhibition can prove these statements.

The exhibition was prepared in close cooperation with the Institute for Contemporary History in Munich. Our special thanks go to the Institute's Deputy Director, Prof. Dr Magnus Brechtken, for academic advice and support. We would also like to thank all the experts who provided their knowledge and their time for preparing this exhibition.

Martina Christmeier/Alexander Schmidt

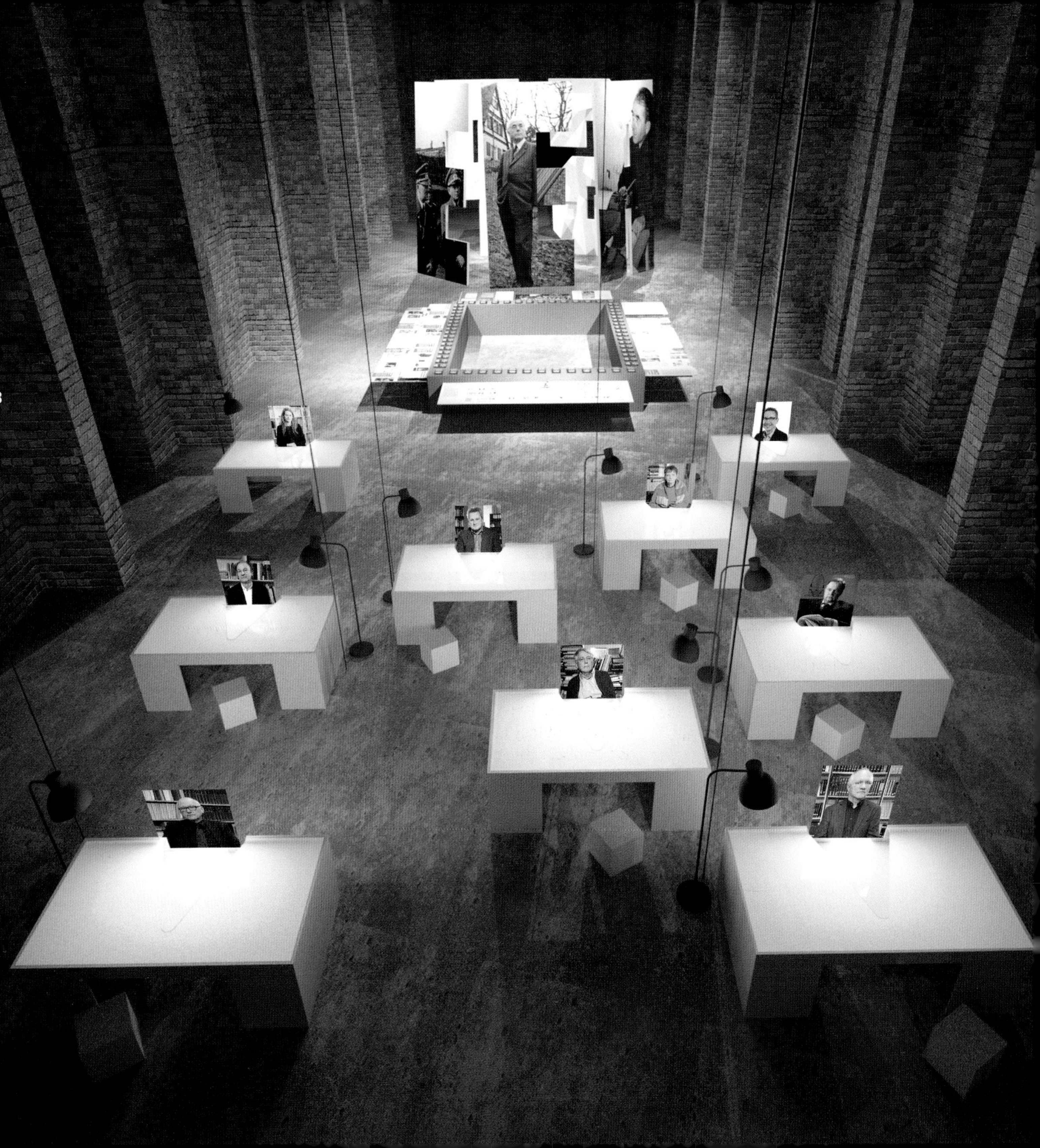

The Design Idea

Speer as Agent

The exhibition kicks off with an installation comprising the five capital letters "SPEER". This construction dominates the room, just as formerly Speer's propagandist view dominated public opinion. The faces of the letters show larger-than-life photographs from various stages of Speer's life: together with Adolf Hitler, during the Nuremberg Trial, after release from Spandau and later on in front of his villa in Heidelberg.

Inside this letter installation, several video projections document how Speer presented himself in public after the war. The figures of speech and lines of argument typical of him are condensed into his pattern of self-justification which, in spite of continuous repetition, seems hardly credible today.

Speer about Speer

The second part of the exhibition is marked by a large dark square with widely projecting exhibition panels. They describe how Speer's legends were established in Nuremberg, how Speer, the seemingly objective eye witness, gained significant attention, how his network helped with this process, and how his PR worked. His books played a decisive role in this – mainly his *Inside the Third Reich: Memoirs* and *Spandau: The Secret Diaries*. Closely strung together in a long ribbon, these books are displayed behind the exhibition panels – but they remain unopened, as a symbol of their dominance since the 1960s and at the same time of their status today as an extremely unreliable resource. Quotations on the inner side of the square underline that some people also contradicted Speer's statements – albeit in the beginning not much attention was paid to them.

Research about Speer

In the third part, visitors will meet academics as "waiting experts" who are hot on the trail of the Speer myth. You can face them across their desks, while they report the results of their research in short statements. Important documents and publications are presented on the desks.

Each of the exhibition sections translates today's knowledge about Albert Speer into a three-dimensional image. The interaction of all the media, in contrast with Speer's assertions, establishes the true image of a perpetrator at the centre of power who was able to successfully conceal his guilt over decades.

Rainer Lendler
Lendler Exhibition Architects

SPEER as a Brand

Albert Speer almost developed his surname into the logo of the "Speer brand". So for example, on all his books, his name is the most prominent element on the cover. The installation in the exhibition is based on this design.

Albert Speer's Life Data

1905	Born in Mannheim
1923–28	Studied architecture
1928	Marriage to Margarete Weber
1931	Joined the NSDAP and took on smaller construction contracts for the party
after 1933/34	In a very short time, became Hitler's close confidant and most important architect
1934	Commissioned to plan the Nuremberg Party Rally Grounds
1937	Appointed "Inspector General for Buildings" for the remodelling of the Reich's capital Berlin and other German cities
1939	Inauguration of the New Reich Chancellery in Berlin
1940	Visit to Paris with Hitler
1942	Appointed Reich Minister for Armament and Ammunition (Armament Minister), responsible for converting the armaments industry to the economy of total war
1944	Serious illness, unfit for service for months, after his return ordered measures which prolonged the war; simultaneously planning for his own future after the war
April/May 1945	After Hitler's suicide member of the Dönitz government
23 May 1945	Arrested by the Allied Powers
after 20 Nov. 1945	Nuremberg Trial of the Main War Criminals with Speer as one of the defendants
1 Oct. 1946	Sentenced to 20 years' imprisonment
July 1947	Transferred to the Allied Military Prison in Spandau
1 Oct. 1966	Released from prison after serving his term
1969	Publication of *Erinnerungen* [*Inside the Third Reich: Memoirs*]
1975	Publication of *Spandauer Tagebücher* [*Spandau: The Secret Diaries*]
1979	Publication of *Technik und Macht* [Technology and Power]
1981	Publication of *Der Sklavenstaat* [*Infiltration: How Heinrich Himmler Schemed to Build an SS Industrial Empire*] Died in London during an interview tour

SP Albert Speer facing journalists after his release from prison on 1 October, 1966
(Deutsches Historisches Museum [German Historical Museum] 90135_7)

E Albert Speer and Hitler during a weapons' demonstration in the Führer Headquarters Wolfsschanze, 1943
(ullsteinbild 00706935, photograph by Walter Frentz)

E Albert Speer in front of his villa in Heidelberg, 1971
(Photograph: Winfried Rabanus)

R Albert Speer in his cell during the Nuremberg Trial, 24 November, 1945
(Historical & Special Collections, Harvard Law School Library)

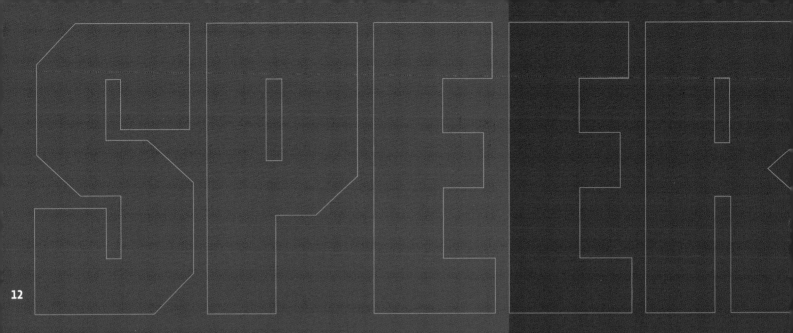

Albert Speer's
Life Audio Tape

In the course of several decades, Albert Speer recorded his "life audio tape"[1]: in innumerable TV and newspaper interviews he consistently repeated exactly the narrative he wanted to broadcast about himself. He literally overwrote the images of the past and phrased his very own version of history. At the beginning of the exhibition, an installation with excerpts from TV interviews and text quotations shows catchphrases and patterns of excuse Speer used to try and justify his year-long behaviour during National Socialism.

Well-known Example: Albert Speer
interviewed by Joachim Fest

The 78-minute conversation contains central aspects of Albert Speer's self-presentation. Fest in his questions offered possible interpretations to Speer. Speer in his answers was very controlled, almost mechanical, and remained very general in his formulations. In his opinion, his only moral error was his general indifference. He never admitted to having been involved in crimes, even claimed that he remained unaware of the murder of the Jews in Auschwitz. Decades later, historians used documents to disprove this.

[1] The metaphor "life audio tape" was first used by Heinrich Breloer in his introductory remarks for a conversation with Leni Riefenstahl. Heinrich Breloer: Unterwegs zur Familie Speer [En route to the Speer family], Berlin 2005, p. 304. Magnus Brechtken later on took up this wording: Magnus Brechtken: "Ein Kriminalroman könnte nicht spannender erfunden werden" – Albert Speer und die Historiker [No detective story could be invented more exciting – Albert Speer and the historians] in id. (ed.): Life Writing and Political Memoir – Lebenszeugnisse und Politische Memoiren, Göttingen 2012, p. 49 & p. 78.

Albert Speer Talks about the Architecture and dramaturgy of National Socialist self-staging, 1970 (Technische Informationsbibliothek Hannover (Hanover Technical Information Library] (TIP))

"It should not have escaped my notice, if I had not thoughtlessly lived for the moment and fled into ever new building plans."

"Now this, as I know today, could only have been about Auschwitz. On that day, I was therefore very close to the secret Hitler kept from us all."

"I avoided this question with the feeling that this was a very monstrous matter."

"Wielding power as such for me was one of the major attractions during this second period of my activities for Hitler."

The Architect. An Interview with Albert Speer
Interview: Joachim C. Fest, 1969
(NDR)

"It was a specific characteristic of that time not to ask questions."

"... so that I felt happy in my group of architects and had the feeling that whatever mean things and dangerous developments and crimes took place outside this group was not of interest to me."

Albert Speer Talks about Architecture and Dramaturgy of National Socialist Self-Staging
Author: Karl Friedrich Reimers, IWF 1970
(Technische Informationsbiobliothek Hannover (TIP))

"Even though he never said outright after 1942 what was happening to the Jews, hints about it were clear enough, so that one could have understood, if one had wanted to, or that I {would have had to understand}, if I had wanted to."

"I would not attempt to deny that I have often acted in an opportunistic way."

The Memory of Justice
Director: Max Ophüls, New York, 1976
(The Film Foundation, Los Angeles)

13

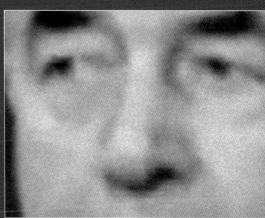
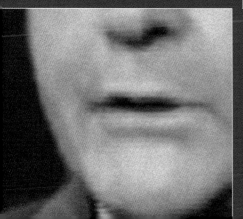

Albert Speer in Interviews[2] (Selection)

October 1966	*Daily Express*
November 1966	*Der Spiegel*
November 1966	*Stern*
October 1969	TV interview in NDR with Joachim Fest
1970	Film Document for Contemporary History *Albert Speer Talks about the Architecture and Dramaturgy of National Socialist Self-Staging*
August 1970	*New York Review of Books*
September 1970	Interview with David Frost
October 1970	*The Listener*
March 1971	*Jasmin*
June 1971	*Playboy* (shortened German version in *Quick*)
June 1971	*The David Frost Show*
1972/73	Conversations with Jörg-Michael Schriefer (published 2013)
1973	Marcel Ophüls: *Memory of Justice* (published 1976)
Autumn 1973	Interview with Uwe Bahnsen and James O'Donnell for the book *The Bunker*
1973	Contribution in *The World at War* on British TV (German version 1975 in NDR)
November 1973	Speer Interview on the BBC
August 1974	Contribution in *Berliner Sportpalast*, ZDF
March 1975	*Welt*
June 1975	*Zeit-Magazin*
July 1975	*Stern*
March 1976	Interview with Dan van der Vat for *The Times*
February 1977	Interview with Daniel Schärer for *Inter Nationes* and further media
1978	*Oppositions*
1978	Interview with Gitta Sereny for the *Sunday Times Magazine* (German version in *Zeit-Magazin*)
1978	Interview for a BBC series about architecture
December 1979	Interview for BBC Radio
March 1980	*The Listener*
1981	Interview with Heinrich Breloer for the film *Das Beil von Wandsbek*
September 1981	Planned interview with the BBC Speer dies in London

This list is based on research by Magnus Brechtken. For details about the interviews and their context see
Magnus Brechtken, Albert Speer: Eine deutsche Karriere [Albert Speer: A German Career], Munich 2017.

"If **I knew nothing, I made sure** that I didn't know anything. If **I didn't see anything**, this was, because **I did not want to see anything**."

Albert Speer in *Quick*, 19 May, 1971.

"I did **not follow this up**. I did **nothing at all**."

Albert Speer in *Quick*, 19 May, 1971.

"Of all these **horrible things** I did in fact **know nothing**."

Albert Speer, letter from Spandau to his daughter Hilde, quoted in *Stern*, 13 November, 1966.

"I only had a **vague inkling**."

Albert Speer in *Spiegel*, 7 November, 1966.

"Well, that was the fundamentally wrong thing at this time, that you **separated yourself from the events** which were **disagreeable to you**."

Albert Speer in *Spiegel*, 7 November, 1966.

"You only felt **responsible** for **your own sector**."

Albert Speer in *Spiegel*, 7 November, 1966.

"... I did **not worry** about that further, and told myself, as long as I was **not personally** involved, this **was none of my business**."

Albert Speer in *Quick*, 19 May, 1971.

"I was in the type of situation which made it possible **to neutralise any criticism**, if I had had any."

Albert Speer, letter from Spandau to his daughter Hilde, 1953, quoted in *Stern*, 13 November, 1966.

"... today I ask myself, what would I have **been able to find out in my high position, if I had only wanted to**."

Albert Speer, letter from Spandau to his daughter Hilde, 1953, quoted in *Stern*, 13 November, 1966.

Nuremberg and Before – The Invention of the Speer Legend

Alexander Schmidt

After the winter of 1944, Speer was already making preparations for the time after the end of the war. The core of his strategy was to present himself to the Western Allies as a valuable military expert, adviser and unique eye witness from Hitler's immediate surroundings. He denied any concrete involvement in crimes.[1]

Glücksburg and Kransberg

In Glücksburg Castle near Flensburg, the last residence of Minister Speer during the Dönitz government, first talks and interrogations with the Western Allies started on 15 May, 1945.[2]

The interrogator at that time quickly identified Speer's strategy: "We found that Speer followed a well-considered tactic of self-justification and of a will to survive. On the one hand this tactic consisted in presenting himself as an excellent technocrat and organiser. He could presume that his enemies would admire intelligence and technical talent (...). On the other hand, his tactic consisted in showing himself completely unconcerned about his own fate. Nobody admires a coward."[3] After his arrest on 23 May, Speer was taken to the prison in Kransberg Castle near Frankfurt, disparagingly called "Dustbin" by the Americans. He continued to cooperate eagerly with the Western Allies.[4] American main prosecutor, Telford Taylor, in retrospect wrote that Speer was "interrogated almost unceasingly" after May 1945, an experience which "in all probability aided Speer in framing his strategy for the trial".[5]

Speer in Nuremberg

In late September 1945, Speer was moved to Nuremberg and was indicted in the Tribunal of the Main War Criminals – on all four counts.[6] The Allied Powers perceived him as one of the most attractive personalities among the defendants.[7] When he was called to the witness stand on 19 June, 1946, he at first played the role of the capable technocrat and organiser, as American prosecutor, Telford Taylor, remembers: "Speer's direct testimony required more than a full day (...) For the general listener it was not a great success (...) and largely irrelevant to the charges in the Indictment."[8] The focus was on his allegedly outstanding skills as a supposedly apolitical expert at the head of the armaments machinery. In his function as architect, Speer on that day emphasised his civilian status: "The buildings which I constructed were completely representative of peacetime building."[9]

In all relevant prosecution issues, in particular concerning his central role in the slave labour programme and his responsibility for the construction and operation of concentration camps, Speer concealed his role as perpetrator through misleading claims and diversionary stories. So, when asked by his defence counsel, Flächsner, he replied reasonably truthfully that the system of satellite concentration camps near armament companies initiated by him had been established "so that long trips to the factories could be avoided", but in the same breath he claimed that this was done "to permit the workers to arrive fresh and ready for work"[10]

1 cf. Magnus Brechtken: "Ein Kriminalroman könnte nicht spannender erfunden werden" – Albert Speer und die Historiker, in Magnus Brechtken (ed.): Life Writing and Political Memoir – Lebenszeugnisse und Politische Memoiren, Göttingen 2012, pp. 35–78. Basic writing about Speer: Heinrich Breloer (in cooperation with Rainer Zimmer): Die Akte Speer. Spuren eines Kriegsverbrechers [The Speer File. Traces of a War Criminal], Berlin 2006; Magnus Brechtken: Albert Speer. Eine deutsche Karriere [Albert Speer. A German Career], Munich 2017.

2 cf. Ulrich Schlie (ed.): Albert Speer "Alles was ich weiß" [Everything I Know]. From unknown secret service minutes of summer 1945, Munich 1999, Breloer, Akte Speer pp. 330–336 (notes on Speer's interrogation on 22.5.1945).

3 John Kenneth Galbraith: Wirtschaft, Friede und Gelächter (Economics, Peace and Laughter), Munich/Zurich 1972, pp. 291–2.

4 Cf. Ulrich Schlie (ed.): Albert Speer. Die Kransberg-Protokolle 1945. [The Kransberg Minutes] His first statements and notes (June–September), Munich 2003.

5 Telford Taylor: The Anatomy of the Nuremberg Trials. pp. 449–450.

6 The four counts of the indictment were conspiracy, crimes against peace, war crimes and crimes against humanity. cf. final summation of the prosecution in Berloer, Akte Speer, pp. 353–364.

7 cf. Taylor, The Anatomy of the Nuremberg Trials, p. 454.

8 Taylor, The Anatomy of the Nuremberg Trials, pp. 450–451.

9 Speer's testimony at the Nuremberg Trial, Wednesday, 19 June, 1946 in The Trial of the Main War Criminals at the International Military Tribunal Nuremberg, 14 November, 1945–1 October, 1946, 42 volumes, Nuremberg 1947–1949, volume 16, p. 430. Complete minutes accessible on the internet at http://avalon.law.yale.edu

10 Speer's testimony, Wednesday, 19 June, 1946, in Nuremberg Trial, volume 16, p. 440.

18 The concrete reality of life for these labour slaves – hunger, insufficient hygiene, violence, high mortality – remained hidden. Likewise Speer – in completely absurd perversion of the actual conditions – described the underground armament factories ordered by him as clean manufacturing facilities. The mass deaths during the hard work of constructing tunnels without any safety measures remained unknown. Tens of thousands of people died for Speer's projects of underground armament production.

All in all Speer claimed to be completely unaware of the issue of concentration camps. When asked by American judge, Francis Biddle, he euphemistically called a stay in a concentration camp "an unpleasant matter"[11] and answered the question of his defence counsel whether he had learnt about the cruelties during his visits to concentration camps with a simple "no".[12]

Instead of talking about concentration camps and slave labour, Speer preferred talking about his refusal to follow Hitler's order to completely destroy the German infrastructure during the retreat of the Wehrmacht ("scorched earth"), and to a certain extent managed to impress the tribunal. Speer invented a plan to assassinate Hitler and plans to kidnap Himmler, Borman and Goebbels – these fables were without any proof, but because they were mentioned in court, started to develop a life of their own in Speer's post-war tales. In his final statement Speer – deliberately detracting attention from the actual subject matter of the trial and his actual role in National Socialism – warned against the dangers of modern technology in the hands of a dictatorship. He claimed that through "radio and loudspeaker 80 million people were deprived of independent thought. It was thereby possible to subject them to the will of one man" (Hitler) – a global exculpation, not only for himself, but for the entire German people.[13]

Although, in the opinion of American prosecutor, Telford Taylor, "Speer left the stand with his reputation still intact"[14], first of all two of the four judges decided to sentence him to death. Because American judge, Francis Biddle, finally changed his mind, Speer got away with a prison sentence – doubtlessly helped by his civilian performance in court and his clear distancing from National Socialism.

This phase from Glücksburg to Nuremberg was important for the later Speer reception in the Federal Republic. Albert Speer had found a new role – that of the eager eye witness with comprehensive knowledge. He had begun to record his "life audio tape" and continued to reconstruct his life story in thousands of notes during his 20 years' imprisonment in Spandau. So, when he was released from prison in 1966, he was not unprepared for arriving in post-war Federal German society and with his book *Erinnerungen* [*Inside the Third Reich*] in 1969 struck exactly the right note between supposedly tragic entanglement and alleged ignorance which the majority of this post-war society liked to hear.

11 Speer's testimony, Wednesday, 19 June, 1946, in Nuremberg Trial, volume 16, p. 587.
12 Speer's testimony, Wednesday, 19 June, 1946, in Nuremberg Trial, volume 16, p. 444.
13 Speer's final statement, 31 August, 1946, in: Nuremberg Trial, volume 22, p. 404.
14 Taylor, The Anatomy of the Nuremberg Trials, p. 454.

Top left: On 23 May, 1945, Speer and the other members of the last National Socialist Government were arrested. Subsequently, he talked to Allied investigators in Glücksburg and Kranberg and offered himself as expert adviser on armament issues.

Jodl, Speer and Dönitz as Allied prisoners in Flensburg, 1945
(Bundesarchiv Koblenz [Federal Archive Koblenz] Image 146-1985-079-31)

Top right: Speer, together with his defence counsels, during the trial continued to develop the strategy to depict him as an artist, expert and apolitical technocrat. He acknowledged the trial as being necessary, pretended to be reformed and repentant. However, he denied or withheld his actual involvement in crimes.

Speer (centre) and his defence counsel, Hans Flächsner, (right) in a visitation cell, 1945
(Stadtarchiv Nürnberg [Nuremberg Municipal Archive], A65 II RA 241 D)

Below: In the dock, Speer was one of the youngest defendants. Hermann Göring tried to dominate the scene with his attacks on the tribunal. Among National Socialist ideologists, such as Alfred Rosenberg, anti-Semites, such as Julius Streicher, and the organiser of the regime of terror in Poland, Hans Frank, Speer, as architect and armament minister with his civilian bearing and reserve, made a positive impression on all observers.

Dock and defence counsels at the Nuremberg Trial, 1945
(Stadtarchiv Nürnberg [Nuremberg Municipal Archive], A65/I/RA-137-D)

During the trial, Speer's appearance was emphatically civilian, and as a seemingly self-critical defendant he managed to win the appreciation of the tribunal and the sympathies of the courtroom. There were often positive press reports about him. Nevertheless, two of the four judges at first voted for the death penalty, two for a prison sentence. American judge, Francis Biddle, finally changed his mind and pleaded for a prison sentence.

Albert Speer in the witness stand of Court Room 600
in the Nuremberg Palace of Justice, 1946
(National Archives Washington)

American court psychologist, Gustave M. Gilbert, talked to all defendants and also noted down Speer's stories. Gilbert's *Nuremberg Diary*, published for the first time in the USA in 1947 and read worldwide, disseminated the image intended by Speer, that of a reasonable and cooperative defendant who knew nothing about the crimes and only did his job.

Gustave M. Gilbert (right) in the court room with defendants,
Speer at the very left, 1946
(National Archives Washington)

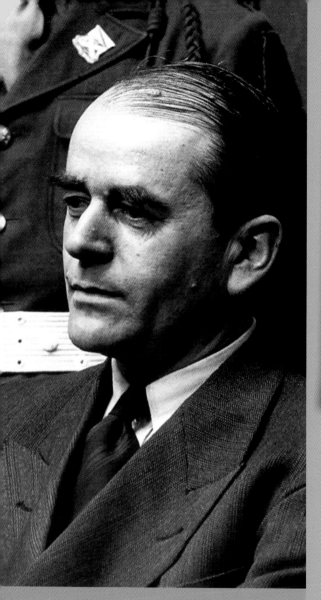

Albert Speer in the dock, 1946
(National Archives Washington)

Albert Speer was sentenced to 20 years' imprisonment for war crimes and crimes against humanity. His co-defendant, Fritz Sauckel, who on Speer's orders displaced about 13 million people to Germany for slave labour, was sentenced to death. For the first time, Speer here succeeded in deflecting attention from his role and his activities as a leading personality in National Socialism.

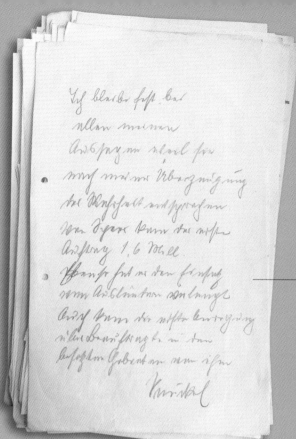

Notes written by Sauckel for his defence counsel, Albert Servatius, 1946 (Bundesarchiv Koblenz [Federal Archive Koblenz], ALLPROZ 3/207)

"I firmly stick to all my statements because I am convinced that they correspond to the truth. Speer gave the first order [for] 1.6 million. He also demanded that foreign nationals be deployed. And the first suggestion about commissioners in the occupied territories also came from him. Sauckel."

"Speer therefore insidiously hoodwinked me. There is no more perfidious act. For he did demand the labour."

Fritz Sauckel was disgusted about Speer's strategy to blame him alone for the slave labour programme. Since his case had already been dealt with he had little scope for correcting this during the trial and was sentenced to death.

Film Documents:
Speer at the Nuremberg Trial

22 In the Nuremberg Trial, Speer during his cross examination and with his final statement attempted to influence the judges in his favour. Here, in Court Room 600 of the Nuremberg Palace of Justice, Albert Speer started his continuous narrative of his version of history – with spectacular claims (not proven by documents and untruthful) and general statements about the dangers of technology and human seducibility.

"Not guilty"
At the beginning of the trial, Speer – like all other defendants – pleaded "not guilty".

Film clip with Speer's plea,
20 November, 1945
(National Archives Washington)

Attempt on Hitler's Life?
In 1946, Speer claimed to have planned a poison gas attack on Hitler in the "Führerbunker", which he had not been able to implement. In spite of the lack of any proof, this spectacular claim was also believed.

Clip from the weekly newsreel "Welt im Bild", 1 July, 1946
(Bundesarchiv Berlin, Filmarchiv [Federal Archive Berlin, film archive])

Skilfully, Speer at the end of the trial did not talk about himself, but presented himself as someone warning against the dangers of technology in the hands of dictatorial regimes.

Film clip from Speer's final statement at the Nuremberg Trial, 31 August, 1946
(National Archives Washington)

Dora Trial in Essen
The legend is continued

Speer as witness in Essen Regional Court, 30 October, 1968
(Bundesarchiv Koblenz [Federal Archive Koblenz])

In 1968, over twenty years after the
Nuremberg Trial, Speer attended court
for the second time – this time not as a
defendant, but as a witness in a trial
about Mittelbau-Dora concentration camp.
Again, Speer deflected attention from
his responsibility for Mittelbau-Dora
concentration camp and took on the role
of the distanced eye witness.

„KOMPLIZIERT WIE VIELE DINGE DIESER ZEIT"
SPIEGEL-Reporter Gerhard Mauz über den Zeugen Albert Speer

Der Augenblick ist historisch, und die Historie genießt den Augenblick. Einer von den Verführern begegnet den Verführten. Doch der Verführer ist längst abgeurteilt und hat verbüßt nach dem Maßstab einer irdischen Gerechtigkeit — der erst jetzt an die Verführten gelegt wird.

Einer, der auf der Brücke stand, von der herab das Schiff in die Strandung gesteuert wurde, und den man dafür bezahlen ließ, tritt in die Verhandlung gegen Männer aus dem Bauch des Schiffes, die erst jetzt hoch- und herausgeholt worden sind, gegen die eine Rechnung erst jetzt erstellt wird.

Die Historie genießt den Augenblick voll Bosheit, den Augenblick, in dem die längst erledigte Rechnung jene verspottet, die noch immer dabei sind. Rechnungen auszustellen; den Augenblick, der die Maßstäbe irdischer Gerechtigkeit dadurch bloßstellt, daß er die nach irdischem Strafmaß erledigte Schuld eines Anführers mit der unerledigten Schuld von Gefolgsleuten konfrontiert. Die Historie genießt den Augenblick, der ihre Interpreten als Spekulanten bloßstellt.

Am 1. Oktober 1946 ist Albert Speer vom Internationalen Militärtribunal in Nürnberg zu 20 Jahren Haft verurteilt worden. Am 30. September 1966 wurde er entlassen. Der Prozeß gegen Helmut Bischoff, Ernst Sander und Erwin Busta vor einem Schwurgericht in Essen hat am 17. November 1967 begonnen, und ein Ende ist noch nicht in Sicht. 170 Zeugen sind der Stoff, durch den sich das Gericht hindurchzuarbeiten hat. Den in Essen Angeklagten droht die Verurteilung zu lebenslangem Zuchthaus. Ihnen wird die Folterung und Ermordung von KZ-Insassen vorgeworfen, die im Harz in Rüstungsbetrieben für den Sieg ihrer Peiniger Frondienste leisten mußten; in Betrieben, die dem Minister Speer unterstanden. Doch wer ist heute der ehemalige Minister Speer?

Da tritt ein altes Männlein in den Sitzungssaal in Essen, bekleidet mit einem Lumberjack von C & A, bescheiden und reinlich — und die Photographen und Kameraleute fallen blitzend und schnurrend über es her. Das Männlein ohne Mantel errötet, dreht den Hut in den Händen, bis das Peloton der Bildjäger erstarrt. „Aber das ist doch gar nicht Speer!" hat endlich irgendwer gerufen. Gelächter. Wer ist denn Albert Speer, heute, nach dreiundzwanzig Jahren?

Dann kommt er wirklich, groß, hager. Das Kommando der Linsen umstellt ihn, er sitzt da im Feuer. Er ist nicht gelassen, er sitzt einfach da. Er ist ein Stück Geschichte, wohl auch schon für sich selbst. Der Vorsitzende belehrt, weist auf das Recht hin, die Aussage zu verweigern, wo sich der Zeuge selbst belasten könnte: „Das ist Ihnen ja klar."

Was ist ihm klar? Ihm ist bewußt, daß er ein Zeuge in vieler Hinsicht ist. Ein Zeuge in diesem Prozeß, aber vor allem der Zeuge einer Zeit, ein Leitfossil; einer, dessen man sich als Quelle bedient, so wie man Dokumente, Scherben und Gebein verwendet.

„Etwas kompliziert" ist das, was er zu erzählen hat, „wie viele Dinge dieser Zeit". Er sagt „etwas kompliziert" und meint wohl eher unbegreiflich, unfaßlich, unerklärlich. Da waren 20 Kommissionen, die unter ihm arbeiteten. Er hat ihre Mitglieder nicht einmal damals kennen können. Denn

Zeuge Speer: „Ich habe öfter mal was verhindert"

„dieses ganze Ministerium war ja eine riesige Improvisation". Und da waren die Intrigen unter denen, die unter der Überschrift „Ein Volk, ein Reich, ein Führer" untereinander stritten.

„Die Sache ist wieder sehr kompliziert, weil hier Zuständigkeitsfragen ausgetragen wurden in der Spitze", sagt der Zeuge Speer. Er sagt das nicht kühl oder distanziert, er berichtet das. Er ist ein historischer Beleg, und immer wieder ordnet er sich selbst unter die Belege ein. „Es gibt ein Buch von einem Mister Irving . . . da stehen diese Dinge ganz genau drin." Er kann etwas nicht sagen, aber das mag daran liegen, daß der Mensch als Beleg schwach ist: „Wenn das nicht in den Akten festgestellt worden ist", dann kann das nicht gewesen sein. Doch wenn das in den Akten stehen sollte, dann trifft das natürlich zu.

Selten einmal spricht Albert Speer von sich: „Ich will mich nun hier nicht herausreden ..." Er kann sich nicht herausreden, er ist drin in der Geschichte; zu heillos ist er in ihr, als daß er seine Rolle mindern, mildern könnte. Nur selten ringt er um eine Formulierung. „Führerprotokolle", setzt er an, „Führerprotokolle", wiederholt er, er zögert und fährt fort: „Führerprotokolle waren Aufzeichnungen, die ich machte nach Besprechungen mit Hitler." Die persönliche Abgrenzung geht unter, ist belanglos. Albert Speer kann der Geschichte nicht mehr entrinnen.

Rechtsanwalt Kaul aus der DDR, Vertreter von Nebenklägern, hat die Ladung Speers beantragt. Er gewinnt einen Punkt für die Anklage: In den Rüstungswerken im Harz wurde die V 2 gefertigt. Dem Zeugen Speer zufolge war die V 2 so unreif, daß es nahezu unmöglich war zu sagen, wann ein Versagen der Waffe auf Sabotage beruhte. Was waren dann die Tötungen wegen „Sabotage"?

Speer war um Besserung bemüht. Hat er nicht gar einmal eine Exekution verhindert, das ist doch in diesem Prozeß schon ausgesagt worden? „Ich habe öfter mal was verhindert in dieser Richtung." Ohne Anspruch sagt das der Mann mit dem faszinierenden Profil, der Mann, den eine Welt von den Physiognomien auf der Anklagebank trennt — und der gerade darum diese Angeklagten und den Vorwurf gegen sie verschwinden läßt.

Der Zeuge Speer tritt ab, vereidigt. Kaum folgt ihm noch ein Blick, denn die Augen starren in den Abgrund seines Auftritts: Was ist diese Mühe um Gerechtigkeit, nachdem sich einer von den Verführern und drei von den Verführten so begegneten?

Article on Speer's appearance in court, in *Der Spiegel*,
4 November, 1968 (*Der Spiegel*, 45/1968)

Speer lied about his knowledge about
Mittelbau-Dora concentration camp which
was established by his order as an underground facility. He had visited the concentration
camp and knew about the murderous conditions there, but ignored them until a medical
doctor urgently intervened. In retrospect,
he claimed to have ordered improvements
which, however, only came much later.

Throughout his entire life, Speer had a distinct talent for marketing himself. Also, after the end of National Socialist rule, he could still rely on an extensive circle of friends and supporters. But that alone cannot explain why his autobiographical narrative, in particular after his release from prison in 1966, met with such wide acceptance in the society of the Federal Republic in the 1960s and 1970s. In order to understand why the Speer legend remained unchallenged for a long time, it is important to take a look at the social context in which Albert Speer's narrative met with great attention.

His success was decisively furthered by the interplay of two factors. The major interest in Adolf Hitler which had influenced the way people dealt with the Nazi past since the end of the war, and the fact that the victims of National Socialist violence only took centre stage in the (west) German culture of remembrance much later with their reports of their own persecution.

Reasons for the Success of the Speer Legend
Unheard Victims and Fascination with Hitler

Hanne Leßau

After his release, Speer encountered a society in the Federal Republic where the voices of victims of Nazi persecution were hardly heard in public discourse. Unlike today, the mass crimes committed by National Socialism were not the focus of collective memory. Instead, media and academia were particularly interested in the person of Adolf Hitler who in the late 1960s and 1970s experienced an almost inflationary public presence. Even then contemporaries talked about a "Hitler wave".[1] The dictator became the focus of interest, both as a private person and a politician, for his person was seen as the decisive factor, even in the academic attempts at explanation of that time.[2] The memoirs of Albert Speer who had been part of Hitler's innermost circle were seen as being of great importance for answering questions concerning Hitler's personality and his political decisions. While the victims of National Socialism gained little attention for their narratives about their persecution, Speer was considered a valuable

eye witness and was much in demand as interlocutor for the Nazi time.[3]

And yet, various initiatives of victims of Nazi persecution had already started to document and publicise their narrative of persecution, some even before the end of the war. The victims did not fall silent about the violence they had had to experience: so-called Jewish Historical Commissions asked survivors to write down their experiences in the early post-war years. Exhibitions created by Nazi victims, newspapers and book publications were intended to make their fate public. People from a Christian-conservative environment persecuted for political reasons to a certain degree found sympathetic ears, more easily in any case than the millions of people persecuted for racial reasons.[4] It was only due to the criminal trials in the early 1960s, in particular the trial of Adolf Eichmann, the main organiser of the deportations, and of the staff of the Auschwitz concentration and extermina-

tion camp, that for the first time a tentative interest in reports by survivors of National Socialist persecution developed.[5]

In the early 1970s, shortly after Speer's death, fundamental changes started in the way people dealt with National Socialism: because of many diverse initiatives, such as those of the "Geschichtsbewegung" [History Movement], as well as due to a changed media landscape, victims of Nazi persecution shifted more and more into the focus. Their fates became a fixed element of a German culture of remembrance.[6] Simultaneously, the explanations of the Nazi rule lost their Hitler fixation and more and more looked at German society: now the focus was no longer on the actions of the dictator, but on the responsibility of the Germans for the functioning of the regime and for its crimes.[7] Both factors also contributed to different questions being asked about Speer's activities. His role during National Socialism and after 1945 was seen increasingly critically.

1 Eberhard Jäckel: Literaturbericht: Rückblick auf die sogenannte Hitler-Welle [Literature Report: A Review of the So-called Hitler Wave], in Geschichte in Wissenschaft und Unterricht 28 (1977) 11, pp. 695–710.

2 Torben Fischer: Article "Internationalisten vs. Strukturalisten" [Internationalists vs Structuralists], in id./Matthias N. Lorenz (ed.): Lexikon der 'Vergangenheitsbewältigung' in Deutschland. Debatten- und Diskursgeschichte des Nationalsozialismus nach 1945, Bielefeld 2009, pp. 217–220.

3 Isabell Trommer: Rechtfertigung und Entlastung. Albert Speer in der Bundesrepublik [Justification and Exoneration. Albert Speer in the Federal Republic], Frankfurt am Main 2016, pp. 122–135; Martin Sabrow: Der Zeitzeuge als Wandler zwischen zwei Welten [Eye Witnesses as Wanderers Between Two Worlds], in id./Norbert Frei (eds): Die Geburt des Zeitzeugen nach 1945 [The Birth of the Eye Witness Post 1945], Göttingen 2012, pp. 13–32.

4 Laura Jockusch, Collect and Record!: Jewish Holocaust Documentation in Early Postwar Europe, Oxford 2012, pp. 3–45 & 121–159.

5 Annette Wieviorka: Die Entstehung des Zeugen [The Genesis of the Eye Witness], in Gary Smith (ed.): Hannah Arendt Revisited: "Eichmann in Jerusalem" und die Folgen, Frankfurt am Mein 2000, pp. 136–159.

6 Frank Bösch: Geschichte mit Gesicht. Zur Genese des Zeitzeugen in Holocaust-Dokumentationen seit den 1950er Jahren [History with a Face. On the Genesis of Eye Witnesses in Holocaust Documentations since the 1950s], in Thomas Fischer/Rainer Wirtz (eds): Alles authentisch? Popularisierung der Geschichte im Fernsehen [All authentic? Popularising History on TV], Konstanz 1998, pp. 51–72.

7 Michael Wildt: Die Epochenzäsur 1989/90 und die NS-Historiographie [The Turning Point of Epochs 1989/90 and NS Historiography], in Zeithistorische Forschungen 5 (2008) 3, pp. 349–371.

In 1946, psychologist, David Boder, who taught in the USA, travelled to Europe. In his luggage: a state-of-the-art wire sound recorder he used to record over 100 conversations with Holocaust survivors. At the time, he was the only one capturing their voices.

Poster shown on the cover of the exhibition catalogue *Fun letzn Chrubn – Taarucha*, edited by Israel Kaplan, 1948 (Staatsbibliothek zu Berlin – Preußischer Kulturbesitz [Berlin State Library])

1945
Unheard

First life reports by victims of Nazi persecution

26   At the end of the war, in 1945, the Allied Powers confronted the Germans with photographs, films and reports about National Socialist crimes. But many Germans were not ready to deal with this evidence.

Correspondingly, there were only very few victims of Nazi persecution, particularly those from the Christian-conservative resistance, who found sympathetic ears for their narratives about their experiences. Nevertheless, Jewish survivors in particular made major efforts to document and witness their persecution.

David Boder with his recorder during his journey to Europe, 1946
(Courtesy University Archives & Special Collections, Paul V. Galvin Library, Illinois Institute of Technology; Voices of the Holocaust Project, www.voices.it.edu)

David Boder:
How came that you got through?

Gert Silberbart:
I was just ... I just was still strong enough to be able to work.

17-year-old Gert Silberbart was interviewed in 1946. Silberbart, together with his family, was deported from Berlin to Auschwitz in 1943 and was the only one to survive.

The poster shows a dead concentration camp inmate, with a scroll and a quill pen, below the appeal to people to document their own persecution stories. Within a very short timespan, the representation of Jews in Germany collected over 2000 life reports with the help of magazines, writing competitions and exhibitions.

German first edition of Ernst Wiechert, *Der Totenwald*, 1946 (Dokumentationszentrum Reichsparteitagsgelände [Documentation Centre Party Rally Grounds])

Der Totenwald [*The Forest of the Dead*] by Ernst Wiechert met with some attention in 1946. The documentary report by the popular writer was his literary way of dealing with his imprisonment in Buchenwald concentration camp where he was taken in 1938 because of his commitment to the ostracised protestant minister Niemöller.

1945
Demon Hitler
Allocating Guilt and Exculpating Oneself

Contrary to their expectations, at the end of the war, the Allied Powers did not encounter convinced followers of National Socialism everywhere. Rather they met mainly Germans distancing themselves from the Nazi regime and seeing themselves as deceived victims. The responsibility for the crimes was mainly allocated to Adolf Hitler and the National Socialist leadership.

In order to exculpate themselves, the defendants in the Nuremberg Trial also tried to paint Hitler as a demon who was ascribed inhuman traits and abilities. Thus for the early stage of dealing with the National Socialist past, Adolf Hitler remained a central figure, even after his death, and had a fascination based both on curiosity and disgust.

Des Teufels General [*The Devil's General*] by Carl Zuckmayer was one of the most performed plays after the end of the war. In 1955, it was made into a successful film. The story of fictitious Air Force General Harras and his pact with "Devil Hitler" triggered intense discussions about the responsibility of the Germans.

In 1945, victory over the National Socialists was staged in impressive images, in particular using Hitler relics. In many places, Allied soldiers smashed Hitler busts and swastikas, carried editions of *Mein Kampf* home as trophies, and posed in places where Hitler had lived and worked.

Destruction of a Hitler bust by a US soldier in Fürth, 1945 (Reproduced from Hugh C. Daly and United States Army, *42nd "Rainbow" Infantry Division: A combat history of World War II*, 1946)

Film poster for *The Devil's General*, 1955 (Walter Koppel and Real-Film GmbH)

1961
Interrogated
Victims of Nazi persecution as witnesses in court

In 1961, the trial of Adolf Eichmann started in Jerusalem. Unlike the first criminal trials of Nazi perpetrators in the 1940s, here the spotlight was increasingly directed at victims of Nazi persecution who took the witness stand. Now their testimonies were no longer seen just as factual contributions to the trial, but were also intended to give the world immediate insight into personal experiences of persecution.

The shattering reports were disseminated in the media, and also in the Federal Republic created a tentative interest in descriptions by survivors. In the wake of the 1968 movement, a critical way of dealing with National Socialism and the acknowledgment of persecution victims increased.

"But I knew that we needed more than the power of conviction of the files; what we needed was a lively testimony of this gigantic human and national tragedy."

Gideon Hausner, Chief Prosecutor in the Eichmann trial in his book *Justice in Jerusalem*, published in 1969.

As one of 110 witnesses, Abba Kovner testified in the Eichmann trial. Because of his active resistance in the Vilnius ghetto, he was one of the best-known citizens of Israel. But also lesser-known survivors got to speak about their fates.

First edition of Dov B. Schmorak, *Sieben sagen aus* [*Seven Testify*], 1962
(Dokumentationszentrum Reichsparteitagsgelände [Documentation Centre Party Rally Grounds])

Within a year after the death penalty against Eichmann had been carried out, a book containing witness testimonies from the Eichmann trials was published. In the next few years, the shocking and horrific descriptions from the trial were increasingly widely disseminated.

Abba Kovner in the witness stand, 1961
(Israel National Photo Collection)

1973
Hitler the Person

A Hitler boom in the media and academia

In 1973, the "Hitler Wave" started, a phase when a huge number of Hitler portrayals by amateur historians and publicists hit the German public. Academic historians distanced themselves from these films and books, but at the same time also strongly concentrated their efforts on the person of Hitler.

As one of Hitler's closest living confidants, Albert Speer was much in demand as an eye witness. His *Erinnerungen* [*Inside the Third Reich*], published in 1969, and his oral narratives were considered to be important sources of information about Hitler as a private person and as a politician.

In 1973, the Hitler biography by Joachim C. Fest was published. In 1977, the film *Hitler. Eine Karriere* [Hitler. A Career] came to the cinemas. Both book and film reached millions of people and disseminated Speer's narrative with whom Fest cooperated closely.

Film poster for *Hitler. Eine Karriere*, 1977 (Interart-Filmbeteiligungs- und Produktions-GmbH, Munich)

> "In view of the abundance of opposing forces, the Führer's will, even if he had intended differently, could finally do nothings else but drive things in one direction or another from case to case, inconsistently and abruptly."

Martin Borzat, *Der Staat Hitlers* [Hitler's State], 1969

> "This man and his intentions and actions will always be the central focus of any Nazi history."

Karl Dietrich Bracher, *Zeitgeschichtliche Kontroversen* [Controversies in Contemporary History], 1976

The dispute in historical science about Hitler's importance in the Nazi state impeded research about other topics. For some, Hitler was important, but by no means the only decisive factor. For others, National Socialism was explained mostly as the implementation of the dictator's world view.

In the Frankfurt Auschwitz trial (1963–1965), more than 200 former inmates of this concentration and extermination camp took the witness stand. Their description of their persecution met with wide media resonance.

Samstag, 11. Juli 1964 / Nr. 158

FRANKFURTER ALLGEMEINE ZEITUNG

Die Zeugen von Auschwitz

Begegnungen in Frankfurt / Zwanzig Jahre danach immer noch Angst / Die Fürsorge des Roten Kreuzes

dv. Anfangs sind die Gespräche von sonderbarer Banalität. Es geht um ein Paar Nylonstrümpfe, die der Mann kaufen möchte, um ein paar Schallplatten vielleicht. Oder um Medikamente — in ganz Polen kann er das Mittel nicht bekommen, nun trägt er es glücklich in der Tasche oder zeigt es befriedigt herum. Die Begegnung mit den Zeugen von Auschwitz, zwanzig Jahre danach, ist eine Begegnung der unausgesprochenen Worte. Was damals gewesen ist, was jene — weiß Gott wie — überleben konnten: es ist nur die stumme, unfaßbare Voraussetzung für alle diese Gespräche, die wir nun mit ihnen führen, nicht ihr Thema.

Im Auschwitz-Prozeß, der seit sieben Monaten geführt wird, sind bisher etwa siebzig Zeugen gehört worden; die meisten kamen aus Polen, einige aus Österreich und Israel. Sie haben ihre Aussagen gemacht: zurückhaltend, unbegreiflich zurückhaltend, sachlich, eher untertreibend als aggressiv, einige ängstlich. Ängstlich? Die detaillierte Rückerinnerung, wie sie hier vom Gericht gefordert wird, erschöpft sie maßlos. Da wird Auschwitz wieder lebendig; und die Furcht, sie könnten hier und heute noch einmal ihren Peinigern in die Hände fallen. Nein, das erscheint ihnen nicht absurd, da doch beinahe die Hälfte der Angeklagten auf freiem Fuß ist. Fordert es nicht vielleicht der Zufall, daß sie am Abend in einer Gaststätte essen müssen, während am Nachbartisch der einstige Scherge speist?

Die ersten dreißig Zeugen, die nach Frankfurt kamen, befanden sich — was die äußeren Umstände angeht — in einer besonders schwierigen Situation. Nichts als die Vorladung der Staatsanwaltschaft und eine Fahrkarte in der Hand, traten sie die Reise an. Bei manchen dauerte die Bahnfahrt 36 Stunden. Dann die fremde westliche Welt, die sich bereits am Hauptbahnhof mit verwirrendem Glanz auftat. Die Suche nach dem Hotel, der Weg zum Gericht, die umständliche Abwicklung aller Formalitäten — und keiner, der dabei half! Mancher Zeuge zog sich in sein Hotelzimmer zurück, von niemandem aufgefordert, Gast zu sein und zu versuchen, sich hier wohlzufühlen.

Inzwischen ist der Mißstand ausgeräumt. Von vielen Seiten wird den Zeugen Aufmerksamkeit geschenkt. Das Deutsche Rote Kreuz in Frankfurt schafft ihnen Schwierigkeiten aus dem Weg. Jeder Zeuge erhält, noch ehe er zu seiner beispiellosen Reise aufbricht, einen Brief, in dem ihm jede Hilfe angeboten wird; dazu eine Liste von Hotels, die, dem Maß des ihm zugestandenen Zeugengeldes entsprechend, für Übernachtungen in Frage kommen. In Frankfurt wird er dann mit einem Brief des Oberbürgermeisters begrüßt und „trotz oder gerade wegen des schrecklichen und für Sie furchtbaren Anlasses" willkommen geheißen. Weiterhin stellt die Stadt Karten für die Theater, den Zoo und den Palmengarten zur Verfügung, der Verkehrsverein lädt zu Stadtrundfahrten ein. Darüber hinaus ermöglicht die Besucherorganisation der Bundesregierung, „Inter Nationes", Reisen in andere deutsche Städte, zum Rhein, in den Taunus oder wohin sonst der Fremde fahren will.

Dies alles aber ist nur Organisation, verwaltungsmäßige Anteilnahme. Menschliche Fäden zu knüpfen, bemühen sich die Mitarbeiterinnen des Roten Kreuzes. Sie laden die Zeugen in ihre Familie ein, zu einem Bummel oder zum Essen. Sie erledigen Einkäufe und vermitteln Privatquartiere. Der freundschaftlichen Wohltätigkeit haben sich eine Reihe von Bürgern angeschlossen, die Einladungen vergeben und herzlich ihre Dienste anbieten. Das geht so bis Hamburg hinauf: ein Pfarrer dort hat eine Blanko-Einladung für alle Auschwitz-Zeugen ausgesprochen, ein Redakteur, der als Berichterstatter von Hamburg nach Frankfurt gekommen war, hat einen Zeugen gleich mit an die Waterkant genommen.

Drei, vier Tage lang sind die Zeugen meistens nur in Frankfurt. Mit ihnen zu sprechen, erweist sich — selbst wenn man Auschwitz ausklammert — als ein weitreichender Gewinn. Rechtsanwälte, Ärzte, Schriftsteller, Journalisten, Architekten, sind diese Überlebenden von Auschwitz unverhältnismäßig stark an dem neuen Deutschland interessiert, wie sie es im Jahre 1964 vorfinden. Die kurze Zeit, die sie hier sind, genügt, das Mißtrauen zu verjagen. Und sie werden zu Hause darüber berichten, daran besteht kein Zweifel.

Bis Ende Juli werden dreißig weitere Zeugen im Auschwitz-Prozeß auftreten. Anders als die ersten, die im Februar zu Wort kamen, wissen sie schon jetzt genau, was sie in Frankfurt erwartet: Sie werden nicht auf sich selbst gestellt sein und überall Helfer finden. Und Freunde. Das mag die Fahrt in die schrecklichsten Jahre ihrer Vergangenheit erleichtern.

Frankfurter Allgemeine Zeitung newspaper, 11 July, 1964
(Archive FAZ)

In March 1964, Maryla Rosenthal was asked to take the witness stand in the Frankfurt Auschwitz trial. For almost an hour, Rosenthal who was born in Cracow in 1908 gave the tribunal an account of her 3-year imprisonment in the Auschwitz camp.

Marlya Rosenthal during the Auschwitz trial, 1964
(picture alliance 89009085,
Photograph: Günter Schindler)

Speer made himself readily available to journalists and historians as an eyewitness. There are over a hundred cassettes alone from the interview project with US-American journalist, Ernest Ostro, in summer 1977, with Speer talking about his life in the vicinity of Adolf Hitler.

Audio cassettes of the Speer interview by Ostro (Dokumentationszentrum Reichsparteitagsgelände [Documentation Centre Party Rally Grounds])

Selection of publications of the "Hitler Wave" (Dokumentationszentrum Reichsparteitagsgelände [Documentation Centre Party Rally Grounds])

Many publications of the "Hitler Wave" were based on Albert Speer's memoirs (*Inside the Third Reich*) or on additional interviews held with him – such as the Hitler biography by Joachim C. Fest. In the 1970s, several quite indefensible books and films about Hitler were also published.

1979
Asked
Victims of Nazi persecution as eye witnesses

32 In 1979, the broadcast of the American series *Holocaust* about the murder of the European Jews reached millions of viewers. It sensitised large segments of the population of the Federal Republic of Germany to the fact that it was essential as a matter of urgency to deal with the persecution of the Jews, and it created increased attention for the reports of Jewish survivors.

In the 1980s, manifold initiatives in society, such as the "History Movement", contributed to the perspectives and narratives of the victims of Nazi persecution becoming a central element in a German culture of remembrance.

Zwi Zydower as eye witness in the TV documentation *Endlösung* [Final Solution], WDR 1979 (WDR/Bundeszentrale für politische Bildung 8WDR / Federal Agency for Civic Education])

In 1979, the documentary film *Endlösung* [Final Solution] was broadcast a few days before *Holocaust* and provided the historical context for the feature film event. More intensely than many films before, *Endlösung* resorted to conversations with victims of Nazi persecution and advertised this.

Dietmar Buchholz (left) talking to former Polish slave labourer, Konrad Krzyzanowski (right), 1988 (*Schaumburger Nachrichten*, 24 September, 1988)

In the 1980s, "history workshops" were established in many places which followed the motto "dig where you stand" and were interested in local history and the history of ordinary people. For these history activists, it was important to interview the victims of Nazi persecution, and acknowledging their experience was seen as a central task.

1996
Hitler's People

New interests and old questions

In 1996, the book *Hitler's Willing Executioners* by Daniel Goldhagen triggered violent discussions in Germany. There was an intensive debate in the media about the role of ordinary contemporaries in the crimes of National Socialism.

With the Goldhagen debate, the change of perspective reached the wider public, a perspective which historical research had established from the 1980s. The focus was no longer on Hitler's actions, but on the question of why the Germans supported him and his criminal policies. At the same time, the major media interest in Hitler's personality continued.

The much-read book *The Hitler Myth* by Ian Kershaw made a decisive contribution to putting the focus on society during National Socialism. According to Kershaw, it was not Hitler's personality, but the propagandist stage productions presenting him as "Führer" and the widespread willingness to follow him which explained his popularity with the Germans.

First German edition of Ian Kershaw, *Der Hitler-Mythos* [The Hitler Myth], 1980 (Dokumentationszentrum Reichsparteitagsgelände [Documentation Centre Party Rally Grounds])

At the same time, the first Wehrmacht exhibition by the Hamburger Institut für Sozialforschung [Institute for Social Research] raised the question of individual involvement in Nazi crimes. It refuted the legend of the "clean Wehrmacht" and promoted discussions in society about individual responsibility.

View of the exhibition *Vernichtungskrieg. Verbrechen der Wehrmacht 1942 bis 1944* [War of Extermination. Wehrmacht Crimes between 1942 and 1944], shown between 1995 and 1999 (Photograph: Sacha Hartgers, Paris)

In the 1980s, a wider public was made aware of the locations of National Socialist violence.

In many places, permanent exhibitions and memorial sites were also established, enlightening the public about local crimes and reminding people of the fate of persecution victims.

Poster of the youth organisation of the German Trade Union Congress, in remembrance of the November pogrom, 1983 (reproduced from: Walter Bauer/Elke Mahlert: *Kennen Sie das andere Nürnberg? Ein antifaschistischer Stadtführer* [*Do you know the other Nuremberg? An Anti-Fascist City Guide*], 1994)

Since the 1980s, the voices of the victims of Nazi persecution have no longer had to struggle for attention, but have met with wide recognition in society. It is now almost impossible to imagine the educational work of memorial sites and schools, but also the media's debates about National Socialism, without the contributions of eye witnesses.

Jack Garfein from France, survivors' meeting 2010 (KZ-Gedenkstätte Flossenbürg [Flossenbürg Concentration Camp Memorial Site])

The new focus of attention on National Socialist society did not end the major interest in Hitler. Sensational news, such as that in 1983 of the alleged find of Hitler's diaries, met with major media resonance. Any representation which promised to promote better understanding of Hitler as a person was guaranteed to be a sales success.

Stern reporter, Gerd Heideman, presenting the supposed Hitler diaries to the press, 1983
(picture alliance 38006578, photograph: Thomas Grimm)

For example, in 2004, millions of viewers watched the film *Der Untergang* [*The Downfall*] which depicted the days leading up to Hitler's suicide as a tragic series of events. Joachim C. Fest was intensely involved in the development of the material, and again had a decisive influence on the depiction of Speer, based on the legend he helped conceive. But now, there were distinct voices contradicting this interpretation.

Film poster for *Der Untergang*, 2004 (Constantin Film AG)

Speer's Network: Builders and Broadcasters of the Speer Legend

Florian Dierl

Albert Speer's professional success during National Socialism and the development of the Speer legend would not have been possible without the support of numerous people. Speer owed his rise as an architect after 1933 to the entourage of Reich Propaganda Minister, Joseph Goebbels, which brought him first important commissions and finally also the attention of Adolf Hitler whose favour decisively influenced the course of his subsequent career.[1]

Prestigious projects such as the planning of the Nuremberg Party Rally Grounds and the construction of the New Reich Chancellery in Berlin resulted in his cooperation with aspiring experts with whose help Speer in subsequent years managed to establish his reputation as the leading architect of the "Third Reich" and as a talented organiser. In his rapidly growing architect's office and in the government agency, established in 1937, of the "Inspector General for Building for the Reich Capital" (GBI), he employed former co-students and experts he headhunted from the Berlin municipal administration. In addition renowned freelance architects and visual artists were integrated into the "Speer System" and were provided with profitable commissions and professorships.[2]

It was particularly the staff of the GBI who had attained executive positions in their profession at an early age and self-deprecatingly called themselves "Speer's Nursery" who served their boss with great loyalty: Speer's unpretentious, friendly and co-operative manner and a payment above the pay scale made it easy for them to identify with their job. The team was absolutely aware of the consequences the planned brutal re-design of Berlin would have, but never questioned this.[3] The "artistic" atmosphere, as it was shown in several cartoons by members of staff, and the fond memories of joint meals and excursions, rather reflected the optimism and awareness of cooperating on an "historical task".[4] This rather elitist attitude was even underlined by Speer's practice of giving his staff direct contact with Hitler at lecture events, and by the repeatedly demonstrated power wielded by the GBI against competing political authorities. Even the criminal dimension of the policy of restructuring pushed by the GBI – the expulsion of thousands of Jewish inhabitants of Berlin from their flats initiated by Speer – was interpreted as a goal-oriented rational solution to a planning problem and meticulously recorded in the office journal of the GBI.[5]

After Speer's appointment as Reich Minister for Armament and Ammunition in 1942, several leading GBI members of staff followed him to the Ministry on Pariser Platz, which had only been very recently established. From his predecessor, Fritz Todt, Speer took on the system of industry organising itself for the provision of army equipment, as well as of procurement of raw materials and further extended it. Speer's confidants were entrusted with key positions, in order to implement short-term,

---

1 Dietmar Arnold: Neue Reichskanzlei und "Führerbunker". Legenden und Wirklichkeit [New Reich Chancellery and "Führer" Bunker. Legends and Reality], Berlin 2005, p. 53.

2 André Deschan: Im Schatten von Albert Speer. Der Architekt Rudolf Wolters [In the Shadow of Albert Speer. The Architect Rudolf Wolters], Berlin 2016, p. 103.

3 Jörn Düwel/Niels Gutschow: Baukunst und Nationalsozialismus: Demonstration von Macht in Europa 1940–1943. Die Ausstellung Neue Deutsche Baukunst von Rudolf Wolters [Art of Building and National Socialism: Demonstration of Power in Europe, 1940–1943. The Exhibition New German Art of Building by Rudolf Wolters], Berlin 2015, p. 100.

4 Deschan, pp. 117, 131, 148; Lars Olof Larsson/Sabine Larsson/Ingolf Lamprecht: „Fröhliche Neugestaltung" oder die Gigantomanie von Berlin 1937–1943 ["Merry Re-Structuring" or The Gigantomania of Berlin 1937–1943]. Albert Speers Generalbebauungsplan im Spiegel satirischer Zeichnungen von Hans Stephan, Kiel 2008.

5 Heinrich Berloer/Dieter Zimmer: Die Akte Speer. Spuren eines Kriegsverbrechers [The Speer File. Traces of a War Criminal], Berlin 2006, p. 90.

38 often improvised reforms and to secure Speer's power base within the numerous organisations under his control.[6]

Nevertheless, Speer only partially succeeded in holding his ground against rival forces in the ministry and against attacks by the NSDAP and the SS.[7] With his staff working on the reconstruction of cities destroyed by air raids recruited specifically from GBI planning experts, Speer created the institutional base for his professional future after the looming defeat in the war.[8] His followers gained valuable experience from a wealth of tasks in central fields of the economy and as privileged decision makers managed to forge links across all levels of the hierarchy. These proved to be useful even after the collapse of the Nazi regime: they mutually exonerated each other from their political past and paved the way for new careers in post-war society.[9]

Even after Speer's sentencing and imprisonment, his former colleagues kept in touch and through their financial contributions enabled the Speer family to survive. From prison, Speer gave instructions to those campaigning for his early release, but they had no significant influence on events. The chance to return to society only came with the end of his imprisonment in 1966: renowned publishers and journalists cooperated in the creation and international dissemination of his publications. The commitment and loyalty of his former companions were in no way honoured in his memoirs. Speer, however, liked to fall back on their exonerating statements when he had to defend himself against critical voices. Many companions perceived Speer's rituals of contrition and his distancing from Hitler as unbelievable and as a betrayal of their common past.[10] The stylisation of Speer (and thus of his role) as the pioneer of a modern, timeless architectural programme nevertheless met with the approval of many and contributed to the public image of the "good Nazi"[11] being perpetrated for quite a few more years.[12]

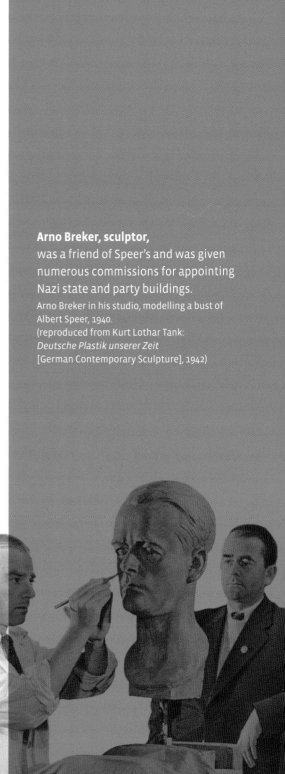

Arno Breker, sculptor,
was a friend of Speer's and was given numerous commissions for appointing Nazi state and party buildings.
Arno Breker in his studio, modelling a bust of Albert Speer, 1940.
(reproduced from Kurt Lothar Tank: *Deutsche Plastik unserer Zeit* [German Contemporary Sculpture], 1942)

6   Gregor Janssen: Das Ministerium Speer. Deutschlands Rüstung im Krieg [The Speer Ministry. Germany's Armament Industry during the War], Berlin 1968, pp. 40, 157.

7   Martin Kitchen: Speer. Hitler's Architect, New Haven 2015, pp. 176, 187.

8   Janssen, p. 230.

9   Nina Grunenberg: Die Wundertäter, Netzwerke der deutschen Wirtschaft 1942–1966 [The Miracle Workers, Networks in the German Economy 1942–1966], München 2006; Richard Tilly: Willy H. Schlieker, Aufstieg und Fall eines Unternehmers (1934–1980) [Willy H. Schlieker, Rise and Fall of an Entrepreneur], Berlin 2008.

10   Deschan, pp. 209, 231.

11   Dan van der Vat: The Good Nazi. The Life and Lies of Albert Speer, London 1997.

12   Lars Olof Larsson: Die Neugestaltung der Reichshauptstadt. Albert Speers Generalbebauungsplan für Berlin [Re-Design of the Reich Capital. Albert Speer's Master Plan for Berlin], Stuttgart 1978; Léon Krier: Albert Speer. Architecture 1932–1942, New York 2013.

1937–1945
Inspector General of Building for the Reich Capital – "Speer's Nursery"

In 1937, the institution of the "Inspector General for Building" headed by Speer and reporting directly to Hitler, was created for the architectural restructuring of Berlin as the "Reich Capital Germania". With his cooperative management style and salaries above the standard pay scale, Speer quickly managed to attract a rapidly growing staff of young, aspiring experts committed to hIm. Jokingly, they referred to themselves as "Speer's Nursery". After 1939, the authority increasingly took on tasks in the occupied territories, as "Building Staff Speer" and "Transport Standard Speer". In addition, later on, Speer's closest associates were taken on in leading functions in the war economy.

Karl Maria Hettlage, lawyer, politician was responsible for the finances of the Inspector General for Building and in the Reich Ministry for Armament and Ammunition. Hettlage's GBI department coordinated the "termination of leases" of Jewish flats in the context of the planned re-structuring of Berlin.
(Bundesarchiv Koblenz [Federal Archive Koblenz], Image 183-H28723)

Rudolf Wolters, architect, was Speer's closest associate and headed the planning staff at the Inspector General for Building; he took on propaganda tasks for the Organisation Todt, and after 1943 headed the staff team for the reconstruction of cities destroyed by air raids.
(Landesarchiv Berlin [Berlin State Archive] E Rep. 400-19; NI W No. 13)

Walter Brugmann, architect, as Nuremberg's Director of Building, headed the planning for the Party Rally Grounds and took on leading functions at the Inspector General for Building, in the Reich Ministry for Armament and Ammunition and in the Organisation Todt.
(Stadtarchiv Nürnberg [Nuremberg Municipal Archive], C18/II-390)

Friedrich Tamms, architect, worked freelance on commissions for the Building Staff Speer and as an employee of the Organisation Todt, on war-time buildings in Berlin; after 1943, he cooperated with staff working on the reconstruction of cities destroyed by air raids, planning for Lübeck and Aachen.
(Stadtarchiv Düsseldorf [Düsseldorf Municipal Archive] 180-660-041)

Cäsar Pinnau, architect, commissioned by Speer, took on the refurbishment of the Reich President's Palais, as well as the interior fittings for the New Reich Chancellery and the Japanese Embassy; he cooperated on plans for the "World Capital Germania" and for the re-construction of Bremen after the war.
(private photograph)

1942–1945
Reich Ministry
for Armament
and Ammunition

40 In 1942, Hitler appointed Speer
as Reich Minister for Armament
and Ammunition and as head
of the Organisation Todt which
carried out construction projects
in the occupied territories.
Thus Speer now held a central
position in the Nazi regime.
With the help of his confidants,
he managed to push through
the independent organisation
of the armament industry
against the resistance of the
Wehrmacht and the public
administration. The informal
network of Speer's followers
continued to exist in the Federal
Republic. Its members assisted
each other with their careers.

Ernst Wolf Mommsen,
lawyer/industry manager,
was responsible for the
departments of War Econo-
my and Procurement of
Ammunition in the Reich
Ministry for Armament and
Ammunition.
(ullstein bild 707439/
photograph: Rudolf Dietrich)

Paul Walter Rohland,
metallurgist, industrial adviser,
was responsible for the rationa-
lisation of tank production in
the Reich Ministry for Armament and Ammunition, and,
as one of Speer's confidants,
headed the Industrial Council
in the Army High Command.
(Landesarchiv Berlin [Berlin State Archive]
F Rep. 290 No. 0119361)

Willy Liebel,
printer/politician, as Nuremberg Lord Mayor promoted
the construction of the Party
Rally Grounds and took on
a leading function in the
Reich Ministry for Armament
and Ammunition.
(Dokumentationszentrum Reichs-
parteitagsgelande [Documentation
Centre Party Rally Grounds])

Willy H. Schlieker,
businessman/industrialist,
in the Reich Ministry for
Armament and Ammunition
headed the agency's group
for raw materials manage-
ment of iron and steel.
(Bundesarchiv Koblenz
[Federal Archive Koblenz], B145
Bild-F013043-0006/photograph:
Egon Steiner)

1945–1966 Sentence and Imprisonment in Spandau

Speer's arrest and sentence at the Nuremberg Trials ended his professional career. In the following years, family members, his lawyer and a small circle of former associates as well as helpers within the prison offered the only opportunities for communication. Friends organised the transport of Speer's autobiographical notes from the prison. Former associates and sympathisers from the social elites of the Federal Republic tried to achieve his early release from prison and supported Speer's family with regular financial contributions.

Hans Flächsner, lawyer, headed Speer's defence in the Nuremberg Trial of the Main War Criminals.

(Photograph: Ray d'Addario)

Friedrich Tamms, architect, supported Speer's family with regular donations to the "school fee account".

(Stadtarchiv Düsseldorf [Düsseldorf Municipal Archive] 180-660-041)

Rudolf Wolters, architect, coordinated Speer's communication with the outside world during Speer's imprisonment and organised numerous support measures, including the establishment of a fund for financial contributions for the Speer family, the so-called "school fee account".

(Landesarchiv Berlin [Berlin State Archive] E Rep. 400-19; NI W Nr. 13)

Paul Walter Rohland, metallurgist, industrial adviser, supported Speer's family with regular donations to the "school fee account".

41

(Landesarchiv Berlin [Berlin State Archive] F Rep. 290 No. 0119361)

Ernst Wolf Mommsen, lawyer/industry manager, supported Speer's family with regular donations to the "school fee account".

(ullstein bild 707439/ photograph: Rudolf Dietrich)

Karl Maria Hettlage, lawyer, politician, supported Speer's family with regular donations to the "school fee account".

(Bundesarchiv Koblenz [Federal Archive Koblenz], Bild 183-H28723)

Cäsar Pinnau, architect, supported Speer's family with regular donations to the "school fee account".

(private photograph)

Hans Josef Maria Globke, lawyer/politician, as head of the Office of the German Chancellery under Chancellor Adenauer, repeatedly campaigned for Speer's release and for this purpose made contact with the Foreign Office and other Federal authorities.

(Bundesarchiv Koblenz [Federal Archive Koblenz], B145, image F015051-0008/ photograph: Renate Patzeck)

1966–1981
Speer as Publicist

42   After his release from prison in 1966, Speer refrained from a return into his profession as an architect. The offer by Berlin publisher, Wolf Jobst Siedler, to publish his memoirs, presented him with the opportunity for financial security and social rehabilitation.

Speer's false depiction of National Socialism resulted in criticism by his former companions, but also rescued some of them from criminal prosecution. Speer was forever anxious to perpetuate his new reputation as "gentleman Nazi".

Wolf Jobst Siedler, author/publisher, cooperated in the preparation of Speer's manuscript with numerous suggestions for change and with his Propyläen-Verlag offered a reputable framework for the publication. He organised the sales campaign for the *Erinnerungen* and *Spandauer Tagebücher*.
(ullstein bild 00016917/ photograph: Harry Croner)

Rudolf Wolters, architect, after Speer's release from prison in 1966, criticised him for his public distancing from the Nazi past. With documents, he supported the exposure of Speer's falsifications of history.
(Landesarchiv Berlin [Berlin State Archive] E Rep. 400-19; NI W No. 13)

Joachim C. Fest, journalist/editor/author, gave Speer advice as his editor, and with comprehensive suggestions for changes had a major influence on the style and composition of the *Erinnerungen* and the *Spandauer Tagebücher*. His publications contributed significantly to the consolidation of the Speer Legend.
(sz-photo 00231459)

James P. O' Donnell, author/journalist, with his publications in the 1970s made a significant contribution to the dissemination of the Speer Legend in the English-speaking world.
(James P. O'Donnell Collection, Howard Gotlieb Archival Research Center at Boston University)

Paul Walter Rohland, metallurgist, industrial adviser, in 1973, in an exonerating letter, worded by Speer, denied that Speer had been present during Heinrich Himmler's Poznan speech about the "Final Solution of the Jewish Question" in 1943.
(Landesarchiv Berlin [Berlin State Archive] F Rep. 290 No. 0119361)

Gerald Gross, publisher, in 1970 published Speer's memoirs for the Anglo-American market, under the title *Inside the Third Reich*.
(private photograph)

Robert W. Kempner, lawyer, publicist, acknowledged Speer's memoirs as a sincere ritual of contrition and as "an important contribution to contemporary history". The former prosecutor at the Nuremberg Trials offered his assistance in distributing Speer's donations to Israeli organisations.

(United States Holocaust Memorial Museum, courtesy of John W. Mosenthal)

Simon Wiesenthal, architect/publicist, was in close contact with Speer over many years and received donations from him. During appearances in the USA, he described Speer as a supposed opponent of war and exonerated him against Jewish criticism.

(Nationaal Archief 932.3671)

The Speer Family

Throughout his life, Speer had a distant relationship with his family. During the years of his professional rise he only very rarely lived with his family in various places. Visits by his wife and children during his imprisonment were usually perceived as a disagreeable event by all involved. The children's development was mainly accompanied and supported by a circle of friends. After his release, Speer concentrated on presenting his view of his own history in public; in the family, his role during National Socialism was never addressed. An extramarital affair contributed to a further alienation between him and his family.

44

„Das ist kein Plädoyer für Unversöhnlichkeit; aber Vergesslichkeit ist fahrlässiger Umgang mit unserer Zukunft. Geschichte entsteht aus Gedächtnis, nicht aus Memoiren."

Dieter Hildebrandt in: *Die Zeit*, 15. August 1975

„Speers Bilanz sieht infolgedessen etwa Millionen Tote, unzählige Millionen Versti Jahre Spandau. Saldo: Zwei Bestseller."

Hermann Gremliza in: *Konkret*, Heft 10 (19

Martina Christmeier

Speer's Media Policy – PR for Himself

After the National Socialists took over power, Albert Speer succeeded in the course of very few years in establishing himself as Hitler's architect and in rising into Hitler's circle of closest confidants. Hitler came to appreciate him especially for his organisational talent, and ambitious Speer hoped to secure himself a leading role as architect. After his appointment as "Inspector General for Building for the Re-Structuring of the Reich Capital" in 1937, he continuously engaged in image politics for himself. With his staff, Speer developed strategies for the public presentation of his plans for the major sites in Nuremberg and Berlin in the shape of specialist articles, publications, films and exhibitions, always linking them to his name. In this respect he was both a producer and a controller of news. Press information was purposefully disseminated, visits to building sites were organised, reporting was meticulously monitored. Early on, Speer established a circle of journalists whom he could bind to himself with exclusive information and invitations.[1]

As armament minister, Speer continued this successful strategy and presented himself to the public as a hands-on, down-to-earth manager who increased armament production to unknown heights.[2] His associate, Rudolf Wolters, organised the press to accompany Speer on all important activities. Speer's portrait appeared on the cover of numerous magazines, photographer, Hanns Hubmann, accompanied him on many of his travels, and made a significant contribution to disseminating the image of the minister as a dynamic "action man".

During his imprisonment, journalists such as Hubmann made sure that the narrative of this Speer image was continued. It was further enriched by the fables launched by Speer in the post-war years, concerning his alleged resistance to Hitler. Even before Speer's release in 1966, numerous articles had established Speer's nimbus as repentant Nazi and saviour of German industry.[3]

When he appeared after his imprisonment, Speer could immediately pick up on the reputation he had established, and the collective world press accepted his narrative. He carefully organised well-paid exclusive interviews with Spiegel and Stern.[4] Carefully considered, he repeated and reinforced the legends which had been put about since the Nuremberg Trial. Alternatively, he took on the roles of the innocent technocrat, the top achiever, the resistance fighter, the man who knew nothing, or the reformed Nazi.[5] Thus in Spiegel, for example, he, allegedly an eye witness, reported on a meeting with Hitler, deflecting attention from the reality of his visits to Mauthausen concentration camp – "as I know today, that was undoubtedly all staged pretence" – and claimed that he only had had "a vague idea" of the things happening in concentration camps. Auschwitz, he lied, had not been known to him. With statements such as "everybody looked after the things that needed to be done in his division, everything else was taboo", he not only exonerated himself, but he also provided an excuse for all those who "only" looked after their jobs and had not known anything and not asked any questions. He laid the blame

1 cf. Alexander Kropp: "Die Presse sucht nach neuer Beute." Medienpolitik und Öffentlichkeitsarbeit des GBI ["The Press Is Looking for New Loot" GBI Media Policy and PR Work], in Dagmar Thorau / Gernot Schaulinski (eds): Mythos Germania. Vision und Verbrechen, Berlin 2014, pp. 76–83.

2 On the supposed armament miracle cf.: Jonas Scherner/Jochen Streb: Das Ende eines Mythos? Albert Speer und das so genannte Rüstungswunder [The End of a Myth? Albert Speer and the So-called Armament Miracle], in Vierteljahresschrift für Sozial- und Wirtschaftsgeschichte, volume 93, no 2, April 2006, pp. 172–196.

3 In 1943, Hubmann accompanied Speer on a journey to Düsseldorf. After an air raid, he photographed the Armament Minister there for the propaganda magazine Signal, energetically helping with clearing-up work. Hubmann presented the same photograph with a similar story in an article in the illustrated magazine Quick on 22 March, 1958, which campaigned for a reprieve for Speer, arguing that Speer, before the end of the war, had tried to prevent the destruction of Germany and to eliminate Hitler.

4 Der Spiegel, 7 November 1966, and Stern, 13 November 1966.

5 On all topics cf. Isabell Trommer: Rechtfertigung und Entlastung. Albert Speer in der Bundesrepublik, Frankfurt am Main 2016, pp. 122–207.

46 for the war "not with Germany", but "with Hitler", and he allegedly felt sympathetic towards the resistance fighters of 20 July, as early as January 1945 – because he claimed he had been in a similar situation then.

At the same time he acted the part of the contrite penitent with a claim to personal absolution: "I have the feeling to be free of the past, after 20 years' imprisonment in Spandau. But I will never shed the burden imposed upon me by the horrific crimes (…) To a certain extent, I have accepted the sentence – in spite of the legal shortcomings the trial had. With these 20 years I have atoned, an atonement corresponding to anything which other people might be able to accuse me of."[6]

Innumerable interviews for magazines and TV followed, all in a similar style and with almost the same content verbatim. In his wordings, Speer usually remained very general, rejecting any blame for the crimes of the National Socialists and denying any knowledge about them. Rather he emphasised his supposed achievements in armament management and his alleged resistance against the destruction of German cities at the end of the war. His sole moral failure, in his perception, was his general indifference to things which were, in his opinion, outside his sphere of responsibility.

Speer thus managed to manipulate and control journalists, publicists and historians worldwide with his charismatic manner. Often he also could rely on old allies.[7] His unique selling point as Hitler's closest confidant assured him omnipresence as eye witness whose reports were believed without any further checking of facts by both the public and the interviewers because of their supposed authenticity. Even the Speer biographies by Gitta Sereny, Dan van der Vat, and Joachim C. Fest, published in the 1990s, largely uncritically accepted his own interpretation and thus failed to consider the evidence currently available. For a long time, the Germans were only too happy to go along with the exoneration strategy of the "good Nazi" which was comfortable for them, too.[8]

Speer's own books made an essential contribution to the dissemination of his legends. In 1969, his memoirs *Erinnerungen* [*Inside the Third Reich*] were published, followed by the *Spandauer Tagebücher* [*Spandau: The Secret Diaries*] in 1975. The driving force behind these publications was Wolf Jobst Siedler, the head of the Propyläen Verlag publishing house. He paired Speer with the publicist Joachim C. Fest, as "interrogating editor". Together these three created the manuscript.

The books became international bestsellers and made Speer a millionaire. His distanced description of the "Third Reich" and his own alleged seduction by Hitler served the Germans' need for exoneration. Renowned publicists and historians – from Golo Mann to Elias Canetti, from Carl Zuckmayer to Alexander Mitscherlich and right through to Robert Kempner – supported Speer's books in [reviews in] the major German print media. Usually Speer's interpretation was uncritically accepted, and his role as contrite penitent was welcomed and believed. Thus the reviews again reinforced the Speer legend.[9]

In retrospect, it can be said that until his death in 1981, Albert Speer managed to keep the confirmatory cycle of his legend going, by multiple repetitions and by skilfully addressing the need for exoneration.[10] For decades, he was able to falsely present his perception of himself and of history as historical truth – worldwide.

6   *Der Spiegel*, 7 November, 1966.

7   So, for example, photographer Hubmann interceded for him several times, cf. footnote 3 and Magnus Brechtken: Albert Speer. Eine deutsche Karriere, München 2017. Biographer William Hamsher was already present during the Nuremberg Trial and at Speer's release from prison in 1966.

8   cf. Magnus Brechtken: "Ein Kriminalroman könnte nicht spannender erfunden werden" – Albert Speer und die Historiker, in: id. (ed.): Life Writing and Political Memoir – Lebenszeugnisse und Politische Memoiren, Göttingen 2012, pp. 35–78.

9   cf.ibid. and Trommer, Rechtfertigung und Entlastung, pp. 74–120. For a compilation of numerous comments on Speer's books see Adelbert Reif: Albert Speer. Kontroversen um ein deutsches Phänomen [Albert Speer. Controversies Surrounding a German Phenomenon], München 1978.

10   cf. Brechtken, Albert Speer und die Historiker, p. 78.

1933–1945
Propaganda Pro

Hitler's architect and armament organiser

As Inspector General for Building, Speer put great emphasis on having complete control of the media reporting about his major projects in Berlin and Nuremberg. But, much to his annoyance, he was often only described as the organiser of these building projects. He therefore continuously made efforts to establish himself as an important architect, in specialist articles, books and films.

After 1942, Speer was equally present on the title pages, as armament minister spurring on industry to supposed new peak performances.

Die Woche, 8 September, 1937 (Dokumentationszentrum Reichsparteitagsgelände [Documentation Centre Party Rally Grounds])

Die Woche, 25 August, 1938 (Dokumentationszentrum Reichsparteitagsgelände [Documentation Centre Party Rally Grounds])

Deutsche Illustrierte, 1 February, 1938 (Dokumentationszentrum Reichsparteitagsgelände [Documentation Centre Party Rally Grounds])

Fränkische Tageszeitung, 19. August 1939 (Stadtbibliothek Nürnberg [Nuremberg Municipal Library])

Hitler was impressed by Speer's organisational skills and obviously saw in him the architect he himself would have liked to be. In a very short time, Speer made himself indispensable as an architect and soon was one of Hitler's closest confidants.

In 1938/1939, Speer launched major press campaigns acknowledging his work as an architect for the re-structuring of Berlin and the design of the Nuremberg Party Rally buildings. However, the beginning of the war prevented the publication of further reports.

Kunst im Dritten Reich, July 1939 (Dokumentationszentrum Reichsparteitagsgelände [Documentation Centre Party Rally Grounds])

Rudolf Wolters, *Albert Speer*, Berlin 1943 (Dokumentationszentrum Reichsparteitagsgelände [Documentation Centre Party Rally Grounds])

Left: Speer's buildings such as the New Reich Chancellery were effectively communicated to the public. The leading medium for the specialised architecture press then was the magazine *Kunst im Dritten Reich* [Art in the Third Reich], with a special issue *Die Baukunst* [The Art of Building] edited by Speer.

Right: Speer perceived himself as a major personality: in 1940, sculptor Arno Breker created a Speer bust, in 1934, Speer's associate, Rudolf Wolters, published an artist's monograph about him.

When work on the impressive monumental buildings had to cease due to the war, Speer nevertheless remained present in the media. The propaganda exhibition *Neue Deutsche Baukunst* [New German Art of Building] organised by him, toured to ten European cities between 1940 and 1943 and provided propaganda for the National Socialist ideology of building.

As armament minister, Speer marketed the increase in armament production as his achievement. He staged himself as a hands-on technocrat and popular manager.

Photographer Hanns Hubmann accompanied Speer. He staged him with his family, and as energetic popular leader. During the "Third Reich", Hubmann's photographs were used as Speer propaganda in the Nazi magazine *Signal* (Speer here shown during clearing-up work after an air raid) and after 1945 in the illustrated magazine *Quick*. Speer also used images taken by Hitler's personal photographer, Heinrich Hoffmann, for his own propaganda purposes.

Berliner Illustrierte Zeitung, 10 December, 1942 (Dokumentationszentrum Reichsparteitagsgelände [Documentation Centre Party Rally Grounds])

Berliner Illustrierte Zeitung, 1 June, 1944 (Dokumentationszentrum Reichsparteitagsgelände [Documentation Centre Party Rally Grounds])

Signal, 1 September, 1943 (Dokumentationszentrum Reichsparteitagsgelände [Documentation Centre Party Rally Grounds], photograph: Hanns Hubmann)

Der Frontarbeiter, 20 April, 1943 (Deutsche Zentralbibliothek für Wirtschaftswissenschaften [German Central Library for Economic Sciences], photograph: Heinrich Hoffmann)

Exhibition *Arquitectura Moderna Alemana* in Barcelona/Spain, 1942 (Arxiu Nacional de Catalunya 340717, 0029)

After 1966
Media Star

The likeable eye witness

After his release from prison in 1966, Speer gave strategically considered information about his past. As in the Nuremberg Trial before, he alternated between the roles of eye witness, innocent technocrat, resistance fighter, man who knew nothing, and reformed penitent.

With his wordings about Nazi crimes, he manoeuvred himself into a distance, emphasising alleged resistance activities and his armament management. Both interviewers and the public accepted his fables as authentic reports and were only too happy to go along with his exoneration strategy.

When, on 1 October, 1966, the gates of Spandau Military Prison opened, thousands of curious onlookers were waiting. A throng of journalists followed Speer to his hotel, and microphones and cameras from all over the world were directed at the Nazi war criminal who was to remain in the limelight for many years.

Albert Speer talking to journalists, 1 October, 1966.
(sz-photo, 602137)

Immediately after his release from Spandau, Speer marketed his stories in well-paid interviews with *Der Spiegel* und *Stern*. This underlined the familiar interpretation of Speer as apolitical technocrat led astray. Critical queries failed to be raised by the journalists.

Der Spiegel, 26 September, 1966 (*Der Spiegel* 40/1966)

Der Spiegel, 7 November, 1966 (*Der Spiegel* 46/1966)

Stern, 13 November, 1966 (Dokumentationszentrum Reichsparteitagsgelände [Documentation Centre Party Rally Grounds])

Even the illustrated magazine *Jasmin. Die Zeitschrift für das Leben zu zweit* published a home story: Speer seemed reformed after his imprisonment, a middle-class contemporary and family man.

Jasmin, 12 March, 1971 (Dokumentationszentrum Reichsparteitagsgelände [Documentation Centre Party Rally Grounds])

Left: In 1971, Speer gave a long interview to the American *Playboy* which, in a shortened German version, was also published in *Quick*: allegedly, he only had ended up in the circle of criminals by accident and because of his official responsibilities, and as soon as he had noticed this, he had distanced himself from them.

Right: Speer often appeared as an eye witness in documentary films, including one by the BBC. His version of history also became the basis for several feature films, such as in 1975 *The Bunker*, and in 1981 *Inside the Third Reich*. The films disseminated every euphemistic cliché by and about Speer.

Playboy USA edition), 6 June, 1971 (private collection)

After some differences of opinion, Speer returns to Hitler. Scene from the feature film *The Bunker* with Anthony Hopkins as Adolf Hitler and Richard Jordan as Albert Speer, 1981 (reproduction in Dokumentationszentrum Reichsparteitagsgelände [Documentation Centre Party Rally Grounds])

52   William Hamsher, *Albert Speer –*
Victim of Nuremberg?, 1970
(Dokumentationszentrum Reichs-
parteitagsgelände [Documentation
Centre Party Rally Grounds])

The first Speer biography was published in English in 1970. William
Hamsher who had already wit-
nessed the Nuremberg Trials as a
journalist, in 1966 reported Speer's
release and then interviewed him
for the *Daily Express* in Heidelberg.
In his biography, Hamsher painted
an idealised picture of Speer and
refrained from checking whether
his answers were plausible.

Gitta Sereny, *Das Ringen mit der Wahrheit.*
Albert Speer und das deutsche Trauma
[*Albert Speer: His Battle with Truth*], 1995
(Dokumentationszentrum Reichs-
parteitagsgelände [Documentation
Centre Party Rally Grounds])

In spite of some corrections to
Speer's CV, British journalist Gitta
Sereny's 1995 biography did not
include the evidence which was by
then available. Her judgment, too,
was strongly influenced by Speer's
own interpretations and by uncritically accepted depictions by other
eye witnesses. In 1978, Sereny had
already published a Speer portrait
in the *Times Magazine* which was
published in German in *Zeit-Magazin.*

Dan van der Vat, *Der gute Nazi. Leben*
und Lügen des Albert Speer [*The Good*
Nazi. The Life & Lies of Albert Speer], 1997
(Dokumentationszentrum Reichs-
parteitagsgelände [Documentation
Centre Party Rally Grounds])

The 1997 book by Dutch journalist Dan van der Vat was the first
not to be personally influenced
by Speer. With his more critical
view of Speer, the author hardly
convinced the German public.

Joachim Fest: *Speer. Eine Biographie* [*Speer.*
The Final Verdict], Alexander Fest Verlag, 1999
(Dokumentationszentrum Reichs-
parteitagsgelände [Documentation
Centre Party Rally Grounds])

For his biography, published in 1999,
Joachim C. Fest mainly used Speer's
own statements and those by other
contemporary eye witnesses from
post-war years. He ignored key
research findings and painted a
picture of Speer which contradicted
available sources.

1969/1975
Speer's Books
Reception and Reactions

Speer's notes and letters from his Spandau
imprisonment formed the basis for the memoirs
Erinnerungen [*Inside the Third Reich*]
(1969) and the *Spandauer Tagebücher*
[*Spandau: The Secret Diaries*] (1975).
Publisher Wolf Jobst Siegler and publicist
Joachim C. Fest cooperated closely with
Speer, both on the content and the style.

The books were a major success, since
they corresponded to a German need for exoneration and picked up on the current debates
concerning Hitler's role. The books *Technik und
Macht* [*Technology and Power*] (1979) and *Der
Sklavenstaat* [*Infiltration*] (1981) were written
without Siedler and Fest. They showed Speer's
stylistic limitations and at the same time con-
stituted intensified attempts at manipulating
history. Their sales figures never reached those
of the earlier successes.

By 1976, in Germany around 300,000 copies
each were sold of the *Erinnerungen* and the
Spandauer Tagebücher. Around 3 million copies
of the *Erinnerungen* were sold, and the book
was translated into 20 different languages.

Through his authorship, Speer secured a
lucrative income for himself: monthly progress
payments, prepublication and film rights as
well as royalties made him a millionaire.

Albert Speer at the launch of the English edition of *Spandau:
The Secret Diaries*, 1976 (picture alliance 26067933)

Top: Fest, as "interrogating editor" had a marked influence on the "much honoured, dear Herr Speer". When Speer wrote his memoirs, Fest's contributions included the suggestion that Speer should describe early doubts about the regime in order to make his later activities look credible.

Bottom left: Speer and Siedler communicated in very familiar tones. But in the end, everything was about good sales figures.

Bottom right: In the English-speaking world, there was a particularly marked discrepancy between marketing and the serious touch, which Siedler and Fest wanted to give Speer's image by emphasising his middle-class civilian bearing.

Letter from Joachim C. Fest to Albert Speer, 22 August, 1967 (Bundesarchiv Koblenz [Federal Archive Koblenz] NL 1340/17)

Letter from Wolf Jobst Siedler to Albert Speer, 14 July, 1975 (Bundesarchiv Koblenz [Federal Archive Koblenz] NL1340/54)

Advert in the Sunday Telegraph for the prepublication of Speer's *Inside the Third Reich*, 1969 (private collection)

Book Reviews from Germany and the USA

Speer's books were reviewed by renowned publicists and historians in all major West German print media. The truth of Speer's stories was hardly ever checked by comparison with archive sources. His interpretation of National Socialism was usually accepted uncritically, his role as contrite penitent was believed and endorsed. Thus the reviews in many cases served to reinforce the Speer legend.

In the GDR, Speer's books were not published. Writer Günter Kunert called Speer's memoirs an "alibi book".

Since there was major interest in the USA in Speer as an eye witness, publisher Gerald J. Gross published his books with great success. Nevertheless here, the press discussed the truth of Speer's statements more critically than in Germany. Taking into account existing specialist literature, the press doubted his self-presentation as a man who allegedly knew nothing. In the USA, Speer was not needed as an exonerating witness for people's own historic guilt.

Elias Canetti

"It was possible to be as close to the source of power as Speer was without being directly confronted with this extermination. This is where Speer's testimony seems to me to be of particular importance."

Elias Canetti, writer and Nobel laureate for literature, in *Die gespaltene Zukunft* [The Split Future], 1972

Hermann Gremliza

"Speer's reckoning therefore looks like this: assets: 40 million dead, numerous millions mutilated. Liabilities: twenty years in Spandau. Balance: two bestsellers."

Hermann Gremliza, journalist and writer in *Konkret*, 10 (1975)

Golo Mann

"Saying that Albert Speer's *Erinnerungen* is the most readable among all those which we owe to the surviving masters of the Third Reich, would not be enough. (...) It will be counted among the top political memoirs, as a most instructive book. Any person who after 20 years' imprisonment was still intact enough to write it, doubtlessly merits our respect."

Golo Mann, historian, publicist and writer, in *Süddeutsche Zeitung*, 20/21 September, 1969

Carl Zuckmayer

"A major book in three ways: in the human attitude of the convicted person; in the firmness and steadfastness of his self-discipline; in the unusual linguistic power of expression whose style is characterised by richness of thought and sincerity."

Carl Zuckmayer, writer, in *Die Welt*, 31 July, 1975

Simon Wiesenthal

"I am just now reading your 'Spandauer Tagebuch', at intervals, because my wife often snatches it from my hands in order to read it, too. I consider this book to be particularly valuable, much more important than your previous book (which we have already talked about)."

Simon Wiesenthal, Holocaust survivor, architect, publicist and writer in a letter to Speer, 16 September, 1975

Frankfurter Rundschau, 14 October, 1975 (Dokumentationszentrum Reichsparteitagsgelände [Documentation Centre Party Rally Grounds])

Open Letter
JEAN AMÉRY
To former Minister Albert Speer
c/o Propyläen Verlag
Lindenstraße 78
1000 Berlin 61

Brussels, 6 October, 1975

Sir,

as a former personal employee of a company which both in a wider and in a narrower sense was also your company (as a concentration camp inmate in Dora-Nordhausen and others), I take the liberty of addressing these lines to you.

For valid reasons which will hopefully be understandable even to you I did not read your books. I will not read them either. It was only through the press that here and there the news reached me that during your imprisonment you had gained insights, had even been reformed to be a determined follower of humanism. *Mieux vaut tard que jamais*, better late than never, needless to say. But, of course, in this very special case, one of the people responsible became aware of the moral facts too late. You, Mr. former minister, did not prevent anything, did not alleviate anything; I was well placed to experience this.

It was also said – I think in a review by Carl Zuckmayer – that you were aware in Spandau that these years weighed less than a single day in a concentration camp. I cannot check the validity of this statement, and I don't have any quantitative measure, since I was not in an Allied prison for 20 years, but in German concentration camps for 642 days. But still I wonder if somebody who reached the conclusions you allegedly did reach, should not have felt compelled to remain silent for reasons of simple human decency. It seems to me that none of the former co-perpetrators has the moral right to go public with moving expectorations. Dignified remorse and profound conversion are only implemented in solitude: without grand gestures in the limelight.

JEAN AMÉRY

One critical exception: Jean Améry, former prisoner in the Mittelbau Dora concentration camp, published an open letter to Albert Speer.

Isabell Trommer

Research, not Fables – Historical Research about Speer

Alexander Schmidt

All those occupying themselves with Speer, did not really have to rely on Speer's tales. The first and best sources were the actual Speer experts: concentration camp inmates and slave labourers were able to testify against Speer's claims from their own experience: a stay in a concentration camp was more than just "an unpleasant matter" (as Speer said during the Nuremberg Trial) and forced labour in the process of moving the armament industry underground at the end of the war was a death commando. Jean Améry, writer and survivor of the Mittelbau-Dora concentration camp initiated by Speer, was one of the few who managed to get his experiences through to at least some of the public. He was not prepared to read Speer's exoneration books and, in 1975, after the publication of the *Spandauer Tagebücher* publicly called on him to finally be quiet, if he was at all serious about his demonstrative repentance.[1]

Erich Goldhagen, in 1970, did not manage to make himself heard with his discovery that Speer had indeed heard Himmler's Poznan speech about the murder of the European Jews.[2]

In the early 1990s, Matthias Schmidt was the first researcher to invalidate Speer's legends by using indisputable sources. His access to the falsified journal of the Speer departments was the basis for a fundamentally different perspective on Speer.[3] This was followed by further research – Angela Schönberger invalidated the myth of the building of the New Reich Chancellery in only one year, Wolfgang Schäche and others did research on the more detailed planning for the re-structuring of Berlin as the world capital.[4] One of these was Susanne Willems, who focussed on Speer's initiative to "de-Jew" the flats occupied by Berlin Jews right through to their deportation, while Heinrich Schwendemann looked at the "unleashed architect" Speer as one of the outstanding perpetrators of National Socialism.[5]

Even the architect Speer was by no means apolitical, as Jörn Düwel put it, but the protagonist of National Socialist building ideology.[6] Jens Christian Wagner reported on Mittelbau-Dora concentration camp, Bertrand Perz on Mauthausen concentration camp and its satellite camps – and on the close links between those camps and Speer.[7] And finally, Isabell Trommer gave a conclusive summary of Speer's reception in the Federal Republic. Magnus Berchtken presented a comprehensive picture of Albert Speer, refuting the Speer legend.[8]

As "waiting experts", the selected authors briefly presented here are represented at this exhibition. In short statements, they answer the questions which Speer replied to in a rather nebulous manner, if at all. Documents from the archives displayed here serve as proof of their research findings.

1   cf. This catalogue, p. 55.

2   Erich Goldhagen: Albert Speer, Himmler and the secret of the final solution in Midstream, vol. 17,8 pp. 43–50, New York 1971.

3   Matthias Schmidt: Albert Speer. Das Ende eines Mythos, Berne, Munich 1982.

4   Hans-Joachim Reichardt / Wolfgang Schäche: Von Berlin nach Germania [From Berlin to Germania], Berlin 1984.

5   Susanne Willems: Der entsiedelte Jude. Albert Speers Wohnungsmarktpolitik für den Berliner Hauptstadtbau [Expulsed Jewry. Albert Speer's Housing Market Policy for the Construction of the Capital Berlin], Berlin 2002; Heinrich Schwendemann: Der „entgrenzte" Architekt. Zur Rolle Albert Speers im „Dritten Reich" [The "Unleashed" Architect. On the Role of Albert Speer During the "Third Reich"], in: Susanne Kuß (ed.): Der Zweite Weltkrieg in Europa und Asien: Grenzen, Grenzräume, Grenzüberschreitungen: [for the 65th birthday of Professor Dr. Bernd Martin], Freiburg im Breisgau 2006, pp. 33–51.

6   Jörn Düwel/Niels Gutschow: Baukunst und Nationalsozialismus. Demonstration von Macht in Europa, 1940–1943, Berlin 2015.

7   Jens-Christian Wagner: Produktion des Todes: Das KZ Mittelbau-Dora [Production of Death: The Mittelbau-Dora Concentration Camp], Göttingen 2001; Florian Freund/Bertrand Perz/Karl Stuhlpfarrer: Der Bau des Vernichtungslagers Auschwitz-Birkenau [The Construction of the Auschwitz-Birkenau Extermination Camp]. Die Aktenmappen der Zentralbauleitung Auschwitz "Vorhaben: Kriegsgefangenenlager Auschwitz (Durchführung der Sonderbehandlung)" im Militärhistorischen Archiv Prag, in: Zeitgeschichte 20 (1993), pp. 187–214.

8   Isabell Trommer: Rechtfertigung und Entlastung. Albert Speer in der Bundesrepublik, Frankfurt, New York 2016; Magnus Brechtken: Speer – eine deutsche Karriere, Berlin 2017.

Isabell Trommer
Political scientist, Berlin

"In the end, you can say that the central justification and exoneration strategies which existed in the Federal Republic at that time were bundled together in the figure of Speer. So the way he was perceived was politicised and shaped by its contemporary historical context. All of this basically only changed after Speer's death in 1981. And it is not a linear process of clarification, the Speer legend was relatively robust."

"How was Speer perceived in the Federal Republic?"

In 2015, Isabell Trommer graduated from the Europa Universität Wedrina with a PhD thesis with the title *Rechtfertigung und Entlastung. Albert Speer in der Bundesrepublik Deutschland* [Justification and Exoneration. Albert Speer in the Federal Republic of Germany] about the reception of Albert Speer. Using press reports and book reviews, she showed in great detail, how Speer was perceived by the public in the Federal Republic between the 1960s and today, and presented the resulting justification discourses.

Trommer works as academic editor in Frankfurt.

Eye witness

Seduced person

Technocrat

High-achiever

Resistance fighter

Person who knew nothing

Penitent

Deconstruction of the Speer Myth through Academic Research

1971 Erich Goldhagen:
Albert Speer, Himmler and the Final Solution

1981 Angela Schönberger:
Die Neue Reichskanzlei von Albert Speer.
Zum Zusammenhang von national-
sozialistischer Ideologie und Architektur
The New Reich Chancellery by Albert Speer.
On the Link between National Socialist Ideology
and Architecture

1982 Matthias Schmidt:
Albert Speer. Das Ende eines Mythos
Albert Speer: End of a Myth

1984 Hans J. Reichhardt/Wolfgang Schäche:
Von Berlin nach Germania. Über die
Zerstörung der „Reichshauptstadt" durch
Albert Speers Neugestaltungsplanungen
From Berlin to Germania. About the destruction
of the "Reich Capital" through Albert Speer's
Re-Structuring Plans

1993 Florian Freund/Bertrand Perz/
Karl Stuhlpfarrer:
Der Bau des Vernichtungslagers
Auschwitz-Birkenau
The Construction of Auschwitz-Birkenau
Extermination Camp

2002 Susanne Willems:
Der entsiedelte Jude. Albert Speers
Wohnungsmarktpolitik für den Berliner
Hauptstadtbau
Expulsed Jewry. Albert Speer's Housing Market
Policy for the Construction of the Capital Berlin

2005 Dietmar Arnold:
Neue Reichskanzlei und
„Führerbunker". Legenden und
Wirklichkeit
New Reich Chancellery and "Führer Bunker".
Legends and Reality

Heinrich Breloer:
Unterwegs zur Familie Speer.
Begegnungen, Gespräche, Interviews
En Route to the Speer Family: Encounters,
Conversations, Interviews

2006 Heinrich Breloer/Heinrich Zimmer:
Die Akte Speer. Spuren eines
Kriegsverbrechers
The Speer File. Traces of a War Criminal

Heinrich Schwendemann:
Der „entgrenzte" Architekt. Zur Rolle
Albert Speers im „Dritten Reich"
The "Unleashed" Architect. On the Role of
Albert Speer during the "Third Reich"

Jonas Scherner/Jochen Streb:
Das Ende eines Mythos? Albert Speer
und das so genannte Rüstungswunder
End of a Myth? Albert Speer and the So-called
Armament Miracle

2014 Dagmar Thorau/Gernot Schaulinski (Hg.):
Mythos Germania. Vision und
Verbrechen
The Germania Myth. Vision and Crime

2015 Martin Kitchen:
Speer. Hitler's architect

Alexander Kropp:
Architektur und Propaganda des G.B.I.
Architecture and Propaganda of the GBI

Jörg-Michael Schiefer:
Speers Vollstrecker – Willy Clahes
Speer's Executioner – Willy Clahes

Susanne Willems/Frank und
Fritz Schumann:
Auschwitz. Die Geschichte des
Vernichtungslagers
Auschwitz. The History of the Extermination
Camp

2016 Isabell Trommer:
Rechtfertigung und Entlastung.
Albert Speer in der Bundesrepublik
Deutschland
Justification and Exoneration. Albert Speer
in the Federal Republic of Germany

Sebastian Tesch:
Albert Speer (1905–1981)

Baijayanti Roy:
The Making of a Gentleman Nazi.
Albert Speer's Politics of History in
the Federal Republic of Germany

2017 Magnus Brechtken:
Speer – eine deutsche Karriere
Speer – A German Career

Jörn Düwel

Professor of History and Theory
of Architecture at the HafenCity
Universität Hamburg

"Although Speer claimed – in retrospect – to have been an apolitical technocrat, this self-stylisation is by no means accurate. For after all, Speer to a significant extent designed the self-staging of National Socialism after it had come to power. This included first of all numerous temporary structures for the staging of major events, followed by the re-design of the Reich Chancellery, a cypher for the authoritarian, 'Führer'-led state, and finally the designs for the re-structuring of Berlin and other cities in Germany, self-confidently displaying a 'New German Art of Building' as an unmistakeable expression of National Socialism."

"Was Speer an Apolitical Architect?"

Architecture historian, Jörn Düwel, works on the links between architecture and its social context, and on the importance of architecture and urban planning for the National Socialist regime.

The volume *Baukunst und Nationalsozialismus* [Art of Building and National Socialism], co-edited by him, documents the creation and context of the exhibition *Neue Deutsche Baukunst* [New German Art of Building]. From this starting point, he deals with National Socialist building ideology.

Megalomania – the German Stadium

The exhibition *Neue Deutsche Baukunst* also presented a model eight metres long of the German Stadium planned as part of the Nuremberg Party Rally Grounds. The "world's largest stadium", like other major building projects, was an important element of propaganda: through architecture, the greatness and claim to power of the "Third Reich" were to be symbolised, but often it simply marked the transition to megalomania in Speer's planning.

Commissioned by Speer, numerous model photographs, drawings, paintings, and even a full scale wooden model of parts of the stands were produced. The project only progressed as far as the excavation, today's Silbersee lake.

German Stadium
with individual
visitors, painting by
Otto Hirth, around
1936
(Dokumentations-
zentrum Reichs-
parteitagsgelände
[Documentation
Centre Party Rally
Grounds])

Left: Prisoners in the Flossenbürg quarry, around 1943 /NIOD (Instituut voor Oorlogs-, Holocaust- en Genocid- studies 67141)

Right: Reproduction from *Die Kunst im Deutschen Reich* [Art in the Third Reich], July 1939 (Dokumentationszentrum Reichsparteitagsgelände [Documentation Centre Party Rally Grounds])

Crimes – Granite from Concentration Camps

Speer's major building projects required significant amounts of natural stone, mainly granite. In order to save costs and increase production, Speer financed the SS-owned economic enterprise "Deutsche Erd- und Steinwerke GmbH" [German Earth and Stone Works] (DESt) which operated quarries using the forced labour of concentration camp prisoners. First deliveries from the Flossenbürg, Mauthausen, Natz- weiler and Groß-Rosen concentration camps for the German Stadium are documented. Thousands of prisoners perished in the quarries under in- humane conditions.

Legend – Construction of the Reich Chancellery in Only One Year

Speer's New Reich Chancellery in Berlin was one of the few National Socialist state building projects which were actually com- pleted. The architecture of power showed essential elements of Nazi ideology. For decades, the legend persisted that the con- struction time was just over one year, which was refuted by Angela Schönberger in 1981.

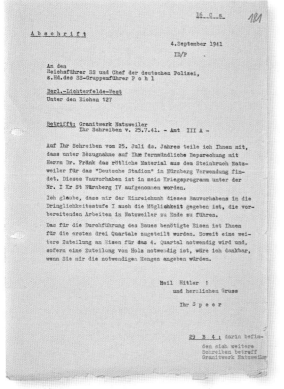

Left: Letter by Albert Speer to Himmler concerning granite production for the German Stadium from Natzweiler, 1941 (Bundesarchiv Berlin [Federal Archive Berlin] R 4606/25, sheet 181)

Right: Letterhead "Granitwerk Flossenbürg" [Flossenbürg Granite Works] naming other DESt works, 1943 (KZ-Gedenkstätte Flossenbürg [Flossenbürg Memorial Site])

Bertrand Perz

Professor for Contemporary History
at Vienna University

"Speer, personally, was not only someone who was completely informed about the concentration camps, because of his visits to camps and his manifold involvement, he was also one of the central agents responsible for the deployment of concentration camp prisoners for slave labour. And, if you look at Auschwitz, he was also directly involved in the mass murder of European Jews through the extension of the Auschwitz-Birkenau extermination camp."

"What Did Speer Have to Do with the Concentration Camps?"

Bertrand Perz's research topics include the history of German concentration camps. Perz also documented and did research on the visits by Speer and others to Mauthausen concentration camp.

His discovery of the extension plans for Auschwitz concentration camp in the Prague Archive for Military History documented the plans for the allocation of slave labourers which were harmonised between Speer and the SS during this time.

On 15 September, 1942, at a meeting with Oswald Pohl and others, Speer personally authorised the extension programme for Auschwitz at a cost of 13.7 million Reichsmarks.

Minutes of a meeting with Albert Speer and Oswald Pohl, 16 September, 1942 (Bundesarchiv Berlin [Federal Archive Berlin] NS 19/14 Sheets 131 and 132)

Auschwitz

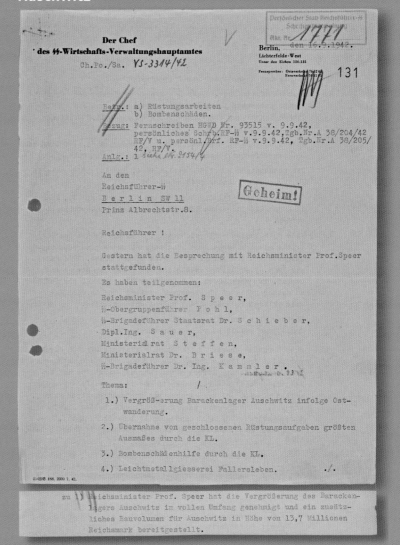

Joachim C. Fest:
Did you ever hear the name Auschwitz during that time?

Albert Speer:
I did not directly hear it.

Albert Speer in an interview with Joachim C. Fest, 1969

Site plan of Auschwitz concentration camp, with the additional buildings and camp areas marked in red, 6 October, 1942 (Vojenský ústřední archiv (Prague), Organisation Todt (1943–1945), box No. 8, inv. No. 31)

In 1942, Auschwitz was to be extended to a central distribution station for concentration camp prisoners for the armament industry – including the murder in so-called "special treatment" of people who were not fit for work. The site plan was an appendix to the SS building application with a budget of 13.7 million Reichsmarks. The file had the title "Vorhaben Kriegsgefangenenlager Auschwitz (Durchführung der Sonderbehandlung) [Project POW Camp Auschwitz (Execution of Special Treatment)]. In internal communications, this project was also called "Sonderprogramm Prof. Speer" [Special Programme Prof. Speer], a direct consequence of Speer's authorisation for the funding in September.

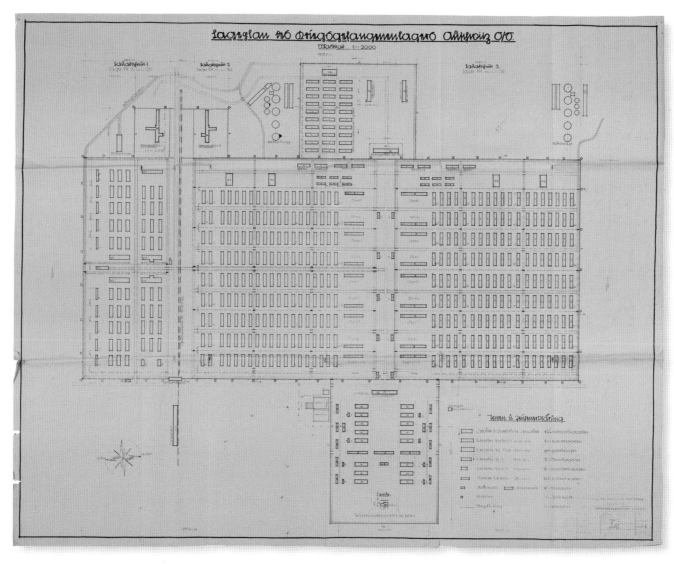

Letter from Speer to Heinrich Himmler, 30 May, 1943
(Bundesarchiv Berlin [Federal Archive Berlin] NS 16/8 ́994)

- 2 -

Diese Baueisenmengen sind nur für den Ausbau
der KZ-Lager, insbesondere Auschwitz, zu verwenden.
Für zusätzliche Behelfsbaumaßnahmen für die Aufstel-
lung neuer Divisionen der Waffen-SS kann ich leider
keine weitere Baueisenmengen zuteilen. Der Bedarf
muß aus den im Rahmen des Gesamtbaueisenkontingentes
des GB-Bau an die SS zugeteilten Mengen entnommen werden. Die Einzelfragen der Zuteilung werden zwischen
Ihren Dienststellen und meiner Rohstoffstelle gere-
gelt. Die Beschaffung der Bezugscheine für 1 ooo t
Gußrohre, sowie der Versand der Wasserleitungsrohre
ist bereits in die Wege geleitet.

Heil Hitler!

64

Linz and Mauthausen

During a visit to Mauthausen concentration camp, Speer presumed that the building measures were too extensive and sent some members of staff to inspect the works. They reported back to him – in particular about Auschwitz where during their visits hundreds of people were killed by gas. Speer's suspicion of wasteful use of materials was not confirmed. In handwriting, he added "that the visit to the other concentration camps yielded an absolutely positive impression."

In the beginning, Mauthausen was important for the architect as a supplier of granite, later on for armament minister Speer, as a supplier of slave labour. In 1944, Speer met concentration camp prisoners in the Reichswerke Hermann Göring in Linz. While this is the only known photograph, it was by no means the only encounter with prisoners and with the conditions in concentration camps.

*31 March 1943
Reich Minister Speer, Gauleiter and Reich Representative Eigruber (...) visited Mauthausen and Gusen concentration camps.*

*6 July, 1944
Reich Minister Speer visited the KLM (Mauthausen concentration camp)*

Activity report by the head of administration in Mauthausen concentration camp, entries from 1943 and 1944
(Archives nationales [National Archives], Paris, inventory 88 AJ, quoted from Bertrand Perz: *Verwaltete Gewalt. Der Tätigkeitsbericht des Verwaltungsführers im Konzentrationslager Mauthausen 1941 bis 1944 [Administered Violence. The activity report of the head of administration in Mauthausen concentration camp 1941–1944],* Vienna 2013)

"Recently, Der Spiegel magazine published your photograph from the Linz steel works with a sneering caption. Here an interpretation of the photograph would be helpful. Maybe like this: these concentration camp prisoners in no way corresponded to the usual picture {of concentration camp inmates}. These were well-nourished and had fresh eyes. Albert Speer asked them to form a semi-circle, with a smile he told them they did not have to stand to attention. He asked them in a friendly voice whether they were happy with their work, their food, but mainly with their treatment. They answered without hesitation and with a smile that they were very well in the works (...)"

Letter from Albert Speer to Hanns Hubmann, 5 December, 1975. Hubmann later took up this story, originating with Speer, in his autobiography *Augenzeuge 1933–1945* [Eye Witness 1933–1945]. (Transcript of letter by Magnus Brechtken, January 2016.)

Gauleiter August Eigruber (centre) and Albert Speer with concentration camp prisoners, 25 June, 1944 (KZ-Gedenkstätte Mauthausen [Mauthausen Memorial Site], Fotoarchiv P/13/14/1, photograph: Hanns Hubmann)

Jens-Christian Wagner

Head of the Foundation for Memorial Sites in Lower Saxony

Before his current post, Jens-Christian Wagner was head of the Mittelbau-Dora memorial site. He has worked on the topic of slave labour and on the role of Albert Speer.

His dissertation *Produktion des Todes. Das KZ Mittelbau-Dora* [Production of Death. The Mittelbau-Dora Concentration Camp] gives a comprehensive report about the history of Mittelbau-Dora concentration camp with its inhumane working conditions underground.

"Albert Speer was basically the great coordinator of deployment of concentration camp prisoners for slave labour with tens, if not hundreds of thousands of victims after 1942 (...) These documents lead to the unambiguous conclusion that Speer was able to assert himself against the SS whenever the interests of the armament industry or his own interest and that of the armament ministry were at stake."

"What Role Did Speer Play in the Deployment of Slave Labour?"

Summary minutes of the founding meeting of the "Mittelwerk GmbH" on 21 September, 1943 (Bundesarchiv Berlin [Federal Archive Berlin] R 121/405)

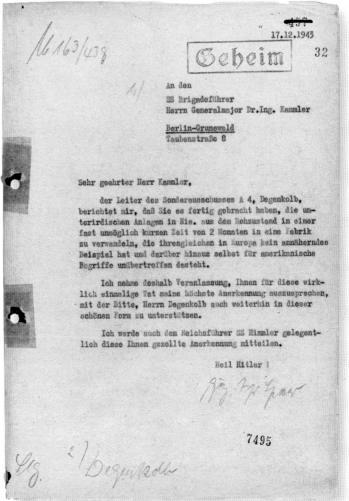

The concentration camp works Mittelbau-Dora in the tunnel system of the "Wirtschaftliche Forschungsgesellschaft" [Economic Research Association] "WiFo" was organised as a state-owned company "Mittelwerk GmbH" and was financed by Speer's armament ministry. Karl-Maria Hettlage, an important Speer associate, was one of the central agents. Around 20,000 prisoners perished in the camp complex of Mittelbau and the satellite camps.

In 1943, Albert Speer personally praised Hans Kammler, head of the "SS Building Industry" for his efforts on the construction of Mittelbau-Dora concentration camp near the "Nie." (Niedersachswerfen) locality. There is no mention of conditions in the concentration camp.

Letter from Speer to Kammler, 17 December, 1943 (Bundesarchiv Berlin [Federal Archive Berlin] R 3/1585, sheet 32)

A series of pictures by Walter Frentz was supposed to illustrate the allegedly clean and orderly production of rockets in Mittelbau-Dora, but in passing, the murderous slave labour during construction of the tunnels was also included in the pictures.

Prisoners connecting cables for the V2 and construction of tunnels in Mittelbau-Dora, May–July 1944 (Hanns-Peter Frentz, Berlin, photographs: Walter Frentz)

"This equipment required perfect conditions of work – air which was dry and free from dust, good lighting facilities, big fresh air installations, so that the conditions which applied to such a subterranean factory would be about the same as those on a night shift in a regular industry."

Speer's euphemistic testimony, Wednesday, 19 June, 1946, in Nuremberg Trial, volume 16, p. 443

Susanne Willems
Historian, Berlin

"When taking decisions as Director General for Building, Speer always linked his interests with the possibility of discriminating against Jews, making him a racist politician. It was not necessary to link the re-structuring project for the city to the persecution of the Jews, but Speer did so to further his own interests."

"Was Speer Involved in the Persecution of the Jews?"

Historian, Susanne Willems, PhD, worked on Albert Speer's policy of pauperising and forcible relocation of Berlin Jews and his involvement in the extension of Auschwitz concentration camp as the hub of a Europe-wide market for slave labour.

In 2002, her study *Der entsiedelte Jude. Albert Speer's Wohnungsmarktpolitik für den Berliner Hauptstadtbau* [Expulsed Jewry. Albert Speer's Housing Market Policy for the Construction of the Capital Berlin] was published, followed in 2015 by her book *Auschwitz. Die Geschichte des Vernichtungslagers* [Auschwitz. The History of the Extermination Camp].

Right: Excerpt from [the minutes of] a meeting of Albert Speer with representatives of [Berlin] municipal administration, 14 September, 1938
(Bundesarchiv Berlin [Federal Archive Berlin] R 4606/157)

Hitler's ideas for a re-structuring of Berlin, pursued for years, in 1937 resulted in the appointment of Albert Speer as "Inspector General for Building for the Reich Capital". Monumental buildings for prestigious official functions and administration as well as striking boulevards were supposed to form the centre of the future "world capital". According to these plans, existing structures in the inner city would largely have had to be destroyed, about 50,000 houses would have had to be demolished and 150,000 people rehoused.

In September 1938, even before the November pogrom which radicalised the National Socialist policies against the Jews, Albert Speer linked his plans for re-structuring Berlin with his own measures against Berlin Jews.

In order to procure living space in a short time, Speer suggested that Jewish citizens of Berlin should be forced to leave their "Groß-wohnungen" (large apartments) and move into "Kleinwohnungen" (small apartments) which had yet to be constructed. The flats thus freed should be taken over by tenants whose apartments were to be demolished according to Speer's planning. This plan was, however, not implemented for the time being.

Left: Model for the planned re-structuring of Berlin as Reich capital, 1939–1944. View of the North-South axis, planned as a boulevard, extending from the planned Southern Railway Station via a triumphal arch through to the Big Hall.
(Bundesarchiv Koblenz [Federal Archive Koblenz] Image 146III-373)

Abschrift.   XVII.B.16

StaPla. VII

Niederschrift.
über eine Besprechung beim Generalbauinspektor
für die Reichshauptstadt am 14. September 1938.

Anwesend: Prof. S p e e r
          Dr. Neikes
          Bürgermeister Clahes
          Mag.Rat Dr.Fränk
          Oberbaurat Stephan
          Dipl.Ing.Hoffmann
          "   " Wilhelmi
          "   " Kaiser
          Stadtrat Pfeil
          Obermag.Rat Dr. Müller
          und der Unterzeichnete

XVII.B.16 2.) Hinsichtlich des Baues von Mittel-und Grosswohnungen entwickelte Prof. Speer einen Vorschlag, der darauf abzielt, die erforderlichen Grosswohnungen durch zwangsweise Ausmietung von Juden freizumachen. Es würde dann erforderlich sein, statt der 2500 Grosswohnungen schätzungsweise 2700 Kleinwohnungen zu schaffen. (Die Zahl der erforderlichen Kleinwohnungen ist höher als die der gewonnenen Grosswohnungen, weil damit gerechnet werden muss, dass verschiedene jüdische Haushaltungen in ihren Grosswohnungen auch jüdische Familien als Untermieter aufgenommen haben.) Diese Kleinwohnungen würden am besten in einem geschlossenen Block der GSW den jüdischen Familien zur Verfügung gestellt werden.

Die Überlegung des Generalbauinspektors ging davon aus, dass für die Errichtung von 2500 Grosswohnungen ein Betrag von rd.67,5 Mil RM. mit einer vermutlich von den Abrissträgern aufzubringenden Spitzenfinanzierung von rd. 18 Mill.RM erforderlich sei. Die 2700 Kleinwohnungen erfordern nur einen Aufwand von 24,5 Mill.RM und bedürfen

- 3-

eines entsprechend geringeren Betrages für die Spitzenfinanzierung. Ausserdem ist die Finanzierung der Kleinwohnungen bereits gesichert; mit ihrem Bau könnte im Frühjahr begonnen werden. Damit ist auch die Wahrscheinlichkeit, dass ausgang des Sommers 1939 die Grosswohnungen verfügbar werden, sehr viel grösser, als wenn erst im Frühjahr mit dem Bau von Grosswohnungen begonnen würde. Als weitere begrüssenswerte Erleichterung ist anzusehen, dass die durch Freimachung gewonnenen Grosswohnungen sowohl hinsichtlich der Raumgrösse als auch hinsichtlich der Mieten den Erfordernissen einer Unterbringung von Abrissmietern sehr viel näher kommen.

Prof. Speer bat in diesem Zusammenhang um Feststellungen, wieviel Mittel- und Grosswohnungen in Berlin von Juden besetzt sind.

Dieser Vorschlag ist streng vertraulich zu behandeln, da Prof. Speer zunächst die Auffassung des Führers erkunden will. Danach würden die erforderlichen gesetzlichen Handhaben zu schaffen sein.

Report form of the Berlin Office for the Implementation of Re-Structuring, 1941
(Bundesarchiv Berlin [Federal Archive Berlin] R 4606/4638)

72 Due to the November program in 1938, thousands of Jewish Germans fled Berlin every month. Speer secured for himself the right to lease their flats in order to house people from demolished properties. For this purpose, landlords had to report these vacated flats. From 1941, Speer's office, in various "actions" terminated the leases of thousands of Jewish people. They had to find accommodation with other Jews, which in the official jargon was a "Schachtelraum" [boxed room].

Tenants in houses which were condemned to be demolished chose a suitable replacement apartment from the flats on offer, listed in printed "Accommodation Listings", concluded a lease with the landlord and informed the Re-Structuring Office. This office then went about evicting the unsuspecting Jewish tenants.

Excerpt from an accommodation listing for tenants from demolition areas, 1942
(Bundesarchiv Berlin [Federal Archive Berlin] R 4606/4638)

The Law on Tenancies with Jews of April 1939 permitted the Speer authorities to record the entire housing space rented by or let by Jewish people in Berlin. In May 1939, Speer earmarked coveted residential areas in Berlin as "Jew-free districts". In the long term, these districts were to be "completely freed of Jews". If necessary, Jews living there were to have their leases terminated and to be replaced by tenants from demolished houses.

In October 1941, the first deportation train left Berlin, taking over 1000 Berlin Jews to the Łódź ghetto. The record of Jewish-occupied living space in Berlin made by the Re-Structuring Office was made available to the Gestapo for the drawing up of its deportation lists. In addition, Inspector General for Building, Albert Speer, benefited from the deportation of Berlin Jews to camps and ghettos since further living space was vacated.

Overview map "Jew-Free Districts" in Charlottenburg, state of planning 1939 (Bundesarchiv Berlin [Federal Archive Berlin] R 4606/3560)

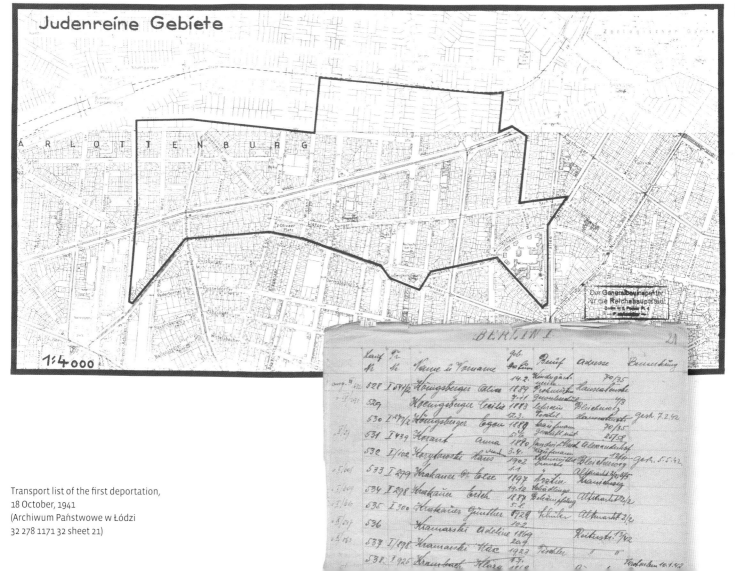

Transport list of the first deportation, 18 October, 1941 (Archiwum Państwowe w Łódzi 32 278 1171 32 sheet 21)

Matthias Schmidt
Historian and entrepreneur, Berlin

„At that time, any renowned historian assumed that Speer really, when it came to the persecution of the Jews (...), the selection of the Jews, that he was not aware of that, that he did not want to be aware of that, and finally that he did not know anything about it. However, now we have journals, and we can see that deletions were made."

"How Were Speer's Falsifications Uncovered?"

In 1982, with his PhD thesis *Albert Speer. Das Ende eines Mythos* [Albert Speer. End of a Myth], Matthias Schmidt heralded a turning point in the response to Speer and fundamentally revised the image of Speer which had largely been determined by Speer himself. He not only revealed the falsification of the *Chronik der Speer-Dienststellen* [Journal of the Speer Departments], but also characterised Speer as a power-conscious careerist who smoothly adapted to any current circumstances.

After his graduation, Schmidt heads a company for economic and investment counselling in Berlin.

Deletion of the Topic "Expulsion of Jews from their Apartments" in the Journal, 1942 (Bundesarchiv Koblenz [Federal Archive Koblenz] NL1318/2, sheet 108)

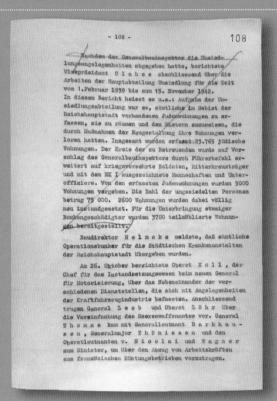

Rudolf Wolters, one of Speer's close associates, kept a *Journal of the Speer Departments* between 1941 and 1944. There were at least three copies of this Journal, and Wolters was able to hang on to one of the copies until after the end of the war. After 1964, he deleted passages which might have incriminated Speer and his co-workers and had the Journal re-typed. After his release from prison, Speer was given one copy which had been expurgated in this way, as well as a summary of the deletions made, and was able to use this Journal as the basis for his books.

Deleted page from the *Journal of the Speer Departments* (reproduced from Matthias Schmidt: Albert Speer. Das Ende eines Mythos [Albert Speer. End of a Myth], Berne/Munich 1982, p. 59)

Letter by Rudolf Wolter to Matthias Schmitz, 11 December, 1981 (Landesarchiv Berlin [Berlin State Archive] E Rep 400-19, Wolters Estate No 214)

Dedication of the first specimen copy of Matthias Schmidt's book, 1982 (Landesarchiv Berlin [Berlin State Archive] E.Rep. 400-19, Wolters estate, No 51)

In 1982, Matthias Schmidt thanked Wolters for his "exceptional contribution" to his book – access to the original copy of the *Journal of the Speer Departments*. Speer's actual role in the persecution of the Jews would otherwise never have been made public.

In 1969, Speer handed over the expurgated version of the Journal to the Federal Archives in Koblenz. At the same time, one volume of the original Journals was discovered in England. Discrepancies were found between this and the expurgated version. When asked by the Federal Archives for the original for purposes of comparison, Speer and Wolters falsely claimed that the original was nowhere to be found.

Disappointed by Speer's distancing himself from Hitler in the post-war years, in 1980, Wolters made available to the historian Matthias Schmidt the original version of the Journal with visible deletions. However, he would not have his treatment of the Journals described as "falsification", but as "abridgement". Matthias Schmith did not accept this euphemistic wording.

Heinrich Schwendemann
Assistant Professor at
Freiburg University

"Was Speer a Criminal?"

"After 1934, Albert Speer depicted himself as an apolitical architect and armament minister, as somebody who had nothing to do with politics. But things were very different. Speer was one of the main criminals in the Nazi system. His actual crimes have been revealed by historical research during the past 20 years."

Heinrich Schwendemann, in the course of his research, produced works on National Socialism and in particular on the person of Albert Speer and his involvement in crimes, both as an architect and as armament minister.

His essay *Der entgrenzte Architekt* [The Unleashed Architect] from 2006 took stock of Speer's crimes and showed his unscrupulous desire for power.

Speer's Crimes

After 1937

Cooperation with the SS in procuring materials for his major building projects in Berlin and Nuremberg: financing of clinker brick and stone processing plants from the Speer budget, loans paid back by the SS via the supply of stone; death of thousands of prisoners in quarries through and for Speer projects.

1938–1943

At the instigation of Inspector General for Building, Speer, eviction of thousands of Berlin Jews from their apartments in order to acquire living space for people from districts which were to be demolished.

After 1942

Order for the deployment of concentration camp prisoners and slave labourers from the East in the armament industry by armament minister, Speer; extreme high mortality in many satellite concentration camps, death of tens of thousands of prisoners.

1942

Personal authorisation for the extension of Auschwitz camp by Speer as head of building.

1943

Construction of Mittelbau-Dora concentration camp for the production of the V2 rocket underground on Speer's initiative; around 20,000 deaths in the Mittelbau-Dora camp complex alone.

After mid-1944

Speer, as armament minister, was the driving force behind the comprehensive expansion of the war economy.

March 1945

Speer's demand for all available forces to "be tough and hold out"; risking the lives of million of people at the end of the war.

Albert Speer speaking in the factory hall of a major Berlin company, for the *3rd Reich Roll Call of the Working Youth*, 17 October, 1943 (ullstein bild 00055227)

Himmler's Poznan Speech – and Speer's Alibi Made to Order

In the afternoon of 6 October, 1943, Heinrich Himmler made a speech to Reich and Gau leaders in the city of Poznan. In this speech he very clearly described the murder of the Jews. Speer was present in Poznan for the entire time.

In 1970, American historian, Erich Goldhagen, in this speech discovered a passage directly addressed to Speer. Goldhagen publicly accused Speer of lying, when saying that he had known nothing about the Holocaust. Speer denied that he had been present. Later on, he obtained affidavits of two witnesses stating that he had already departed from Poznan before the Himmler speech.

"I did not deem myself justified in exterminating the men – that is to say to kill them or to let them be killed – while allowing their children to grow up to avenge themselves on our sons and grandchildren. The hard decision had to be taken – This People Must Disappear From The Face Of The Earth. [...] The Jewish question in the territories occupied by us will be finished by the end of this year. There will be left only remnants of single Jews in hiding."

Heinrich Himmler in Poznan on 6 October, 1943, on the "Jewish Question" (quoted from Erich Goldhagen, Albert Speer, Himmler and the secrecy of the final solution, from: Midstream, vol, 17, pp. 43–50, 1971)

"This whole ghetto produced fur coats, clothing and the like. Earlier when we wanted to get to it we were told: Stop! You disturb the war economy! Stop! Defense enterprise! **Of course all this has nothing to do with [Party] Comrade Speer, you cannot do anything about it.** *It is those alleged defense enterprises that [Party] Comrade Speer and I jointly will cleanse during the coming weeks and months."*

During his Poznan speech of 6 October, 1943, Heinrich Himmler, directly addressed Albert Speer (quoted from Erich Goldhagen, Albert Speer, Himmler and the secrecy of the final solution, in Midstream, vol. 17, pp. 43–50, 1971)

Letter from Albert Speer to Walter Rohland, 2 July, 1973 (carbon copy) (Bundesarchiv Koblenz [Federal Archive Koblenz] NL 1340/49)

2.7.1973

Lieber Freund Rohland,

unterdessen habe ich durch einen Zufall die Einführung und Zwischenbemerkungen Bormanns auf der Gauleiter-Tagung von 6. Oktober erhalten. Ich lege Ihnen eine Abschrift bei. Auch daraus geht eigentlich hervor, dass ich kein Tagungsteilnehmer war, sondern als Gast empfangen wurde. Aus der zweiten Anlage ersehen Sie eine Übersicht über den Terminablauf. Es war mir entgangen, dass die Tageseinteilung ausdrücklich als "Terminkalender" bezeichnet wird, was beinhaltet, dass es die für den Tag vorgesehenen Termin sind, die bei Hitler wie auch bei mir jederzeit umgeworfen werden konnten. Jedenfalls war nach diesem Terminkalender zur fraglichen Zeit keine Besprechung angesetzt.

Merker habe ich unterdessen angeschrieben, er kann sich nur daran erinnern, dass er mit mir Mittag gegessen hat. Danach ist er abgefahren. Ich werde nun auch noch Herrn Schlieker deswegen anschreiben, die Adresse von Frydag allerdings konnte ich nicht feststellen. Vielleicht wäre es gut, wenn Sie bei Ihrer eidesstattlichen Erklärung auf Seite 2 die Zeit (25 Uhr) weglassen würden. Erfahrungsgemäss ist es fast unmöglich, sich an ein derartiges Detail zu erinnern, um so weniger als Besprechungen bei Hitler wegen der Konzentriertheit ihres Inhalts einem oft länger vorkamen als sie tatsächlich waren. Ich würde vorschlagen, dass Sie nach "während der ersten Weltkrieges....." fortfahren: "Als die Unterhaltung beendet war, schien Hitler sichtlich beeindruckt

- 2 -

zu sein....... (Absatz) Da ich nur einmal auf einer Gauleiter-Tagung gesprochen habe und aus den Akten des Bundesarchivs und einem Tonband des Deutschen Rundfunkarchivs hervorgeht, dass ich diese Rede am 6. Oktober 1943 vormittags auf der Posener Gauleiter-Tagung gehalten habe, da ich ferner nur einmal im Auto mit Speer von Posen nach Rastenburg gefahren bin, steht einwandfrei fest, dass an Nachmittag des 6. Oktober 1943 weder Speer noch ich in Posen anwesend sein konnten. (Absatz) Ich erkläre an......"

Ich glaube, dass ein derartiger Satz doch gut ist, um den Eindruck der eidesstattlichen Erklärung zu verstärken.

Übrigens habe ich mir von Flugkapitän Nein in einer eidesstattlichen Erklärung ausrechnen lassen, ob theoretisch die Möglichkeit bestand, dass ich mit Ihnen nach der Rede Himmlers nach Rastenburg geflogen sein könnte. Der Zeitaufwand zur Durchführung eines Fluges von Posen nach Rastenburg beträgt einschliesslich Fahrt vom Stadtzentrum zum Flughafen und vom Flughafen Rastenburg in das Führerhauptquartier zwei Stunden fünfundzwanzig Minuten. Nach der Erklärung Neins war dreissig Minuten nach Sonnenuntergang die letzte Landemöglichkeit vor Einbruch der Dunkelheit. Sonnenuntergang am 6. Oktober 17,53 Uhr.

Abschrift meines Briefes an Schlieker lege ich bei. Ich hoffe, lieber Herr Rohland, dass Sie mir bald die neue Erklärung zuschicken. Zeit braut sich etwas in Jerusalem zusammen! Allerdings von - wie ich bisher den Eindruck habe - fairen Wissenschaftlern, von denen ich mir sogar erhoffe, dass sie die Angelegenheit in einwandfreier Weise klären.

P.S. Vielleicht schicken Sie, wenn Sie es für gut halten, Schlieker noch einige zusätzliche Zeilen. Seine Adresse: Willy H. Schlieker, 8243 Ramsau.

8.5.1973

Lieber Herr Rohland,

um Ihnen die Mühe zu ersparen, meine Wünsche zu erraten, schicke ich Ihnen kurzerhand einen Entwurf für eine eidesstattliche Versicherung. Natürlich will ich Sie damit nicht beeinflussen, aber ich glaube alles ist ohnehin klar.

Sie nehmen mir doch nicht übel, dass ich gern eine solche Erklärung in den Akten hätte. Bei der heutigen unsicheren Verkehrslage weiss keiner von uns, wann ihm etwas zustösst, und Sie sind in dieser für sich peinlichen Angelegenheit der einzige Zeuge, der zählt. Sicher wird mir eines Tages in der Öffentlichkeit massiv vorgeworfen werden, dass ich bei dieser Himmlerrede anwesend war. Nachdem nun glücklicherweise der Fall Ganzenmüller abgeschlossen ist, wird irgendwann eine andere Gelegenheit dazu gesucht und gefunden werden.

Es grüsst Sie herzlich
Ihr

P.S. Die Entfernung von Posen nach Rastenburg dürfte etwa 450 Kilometer sein. Da die Strassen fast ohne Verkehr und auf der ostpreussischen Seite in gutem Zustand waren, wir nicht langsam fuhren, müssten fünf bis sechs Stunden Fahrt ausgereicht haben. Beim ADAC lasse ich feststellen, wie die genauen Kilometerentfernungen sind.

Organised Falsification of History – Sources from the Speer Estate

In retrospect, Speer organised "proof" which was intended to make credible his claim that he left by car after lunch to go to the Hitler headquarters in Rastenburg. Speer's query to the ADAC [German automobile club] concerning road conditions resulted in the response that this journey would be rather difficult, so Speer could not use this answer for his purposes.

He therefore, "as a precautionary measure", asked his old confidant, Walter Rohland, to supply him with an affidavit concerning his absence from Poznan during the Himmler speech – and conveniently appended a sheet with the suggested wording which Rohland used almost verbatim. Speer received a similar affidavit from another confidant, Willy H. Schliecker. A flight captain confirmed that he would not have been able to land in Rastenburg later in the day due to the lack of lighting [at the airport], therefore a flight later in the day would supposedly have to be excluded.

Letter from Albert Speer to Walter Rohland, 8 May, 1973, appended to this a suggestion for wording (carbon copy) (Bundesarchiv Koblenz [Federal Archive Koblenz] NL 1340/196)

Heinrich Breloer
Director and author

"How Did the *Speer und Er* Project Come About?"

In his films, Heinrich Breloer deals with the more recent history of Germany. In his works, which have received numerous awards, he has made a major contribution to the open form of Documentary Drama on German television – a dense montage of documentary research and reconstructions.

In 2005, his project *Speer und Er* [Speer and He] made a decisive contribution to a new image of Speer in the public perception. Together with Rainer Zimmer, Breloer in *Die Akte Speer* [The Speer File], for the first time presented the collected sources on Speer's crimes which had formed the basis for his critical view of Speer in the Film *Speer und Er*.

Heinrich Breloer with Albert Speer, 1981 (private photograph)

In 1981, the young documentary film maker got to know Albert Speer during his research. Without having a lot of background knowledge, he was quickly taken by the eyewitness Speer and agreed to do another project with him. However, Speer died shortly afterwards.

Albert Speer (Sebastian Koch, centre) in the model hall presents his designs for the "new Berlin" to Adolf Hitler (Tobias Moretti, left). Also present: Speer's associate and friend, Rudolf Wolters (Axel Milberg, right).
Scene photograph from *Speer und Er*, 2005 (WDR/Stefan Falke)

On 1 October, 1966, Albert Speer (Sebastian Koch) is released from Spandau after 20 years' imprisonment.
Scene photograph from *Speer und Er*, 2005 (WDR/Stefan Falke)

DVD *Speer und Er*, 2005
(Dokumentationszentrum Reichsparteitagsgelände [Documentation Centre Party Rally Grounds])

In his film project *Speer und Er*, Heinrich Breloer shows Speer's career as an architect, his time as armament minister, the Nuremberg Trial and his imprisonment until his release in 1966. In the documentation *Nachspiel – Die Täuschung* [Epilogue – the Deception], Breloer attempts to trace the construction of Speer's lies and legends, and clearly points out his crimes.

For his documentary *Nachspiel – Die Täuschung* [Epilogue – the Deception], Heinrich Breloer was the first to talk to Speer's children for any length of time. He described this way of working as "filmed research". Breloer asked questions about the guilt of the parents, for himself and on behalf of an entire generation. The interviews were published in the book *Unterwegs zur Familie Speer* [En Route to the Speer Family].

Heinrich Breloer during filming interviewing Speer's children, Albert Speer junior (b. 1934) and Hilde Schramm (b. 1936).
Working images from *Speer und Er*, 2004 (WDR/Stefan Falke)

Magnus Brechtken
Deputy Director of the Institute for
Contemporary History, Munich

*"With the way he positioned himself in public,
particularly after 1966, until his death in
1981, Speer was an ideal projection surface
for millions of Germans who would have loved
to tell the same distancing story about
National Socialism as Speer did (...) That is
basically the Speer legend, and because
it ideally matched the needs of German
society, it was very successful for decades."*

"Why Did the Speer Legend Work?"

The working focus of historian
Professor Magnus Brechtken is the
history of National Socialism,
politics and media, as well as political
memoirs. After comprehensive
research, he presented a biography
of Albert Speer which did away
with the legends, myths and false
representations of previous decades.

View of Albert Speer's country residence
in Altranft, planning stage August 1942
(Bayerisches Hauptstaatsarchiv München
[Bavarian Main State Archive Munich]
Speer Plans 2335)

Siedler's report about the commercial success of the Speer books, 20 February, 1976 (Bundesarchiv Koblenz [Federal Archive Koblenz] NL1340/54)

Speer and Money

Careerist Speer was always keen to make money. In spite of his public offices as Inspector General of Building and later as minister, he pocketed high architect's fees for the state buildings planned by him and had further income, for example from his office as member of the Reichstag or as Prussian State councillor. Speer also dealt in "Aryanised" real estate. His lifestyle was luxurious.

After his release from prison in 1966, he was highly professional in turning his memoirs into money and became a millionaire with these publications. Added to this, there were secret sales of paintings from the years before 1945. Until his death in 1981, Speer led the life of a rich man.

VERLAG ULLSTEIN GMBH

PROPYLÄEN VERLAG · ULLSTEIN BUCHVERLAG · ULLSTEIN TASCHENBUCHVERLAG

DIREKTORIUM

Lieber Herr Speer,

Sie werden wissen wollen, wie es mit Ihren Büchern weitergeht. Deshalb hier ein paar Zahlen.

Von der Buchausgabe der "Erinnerungen" wurden im letzten Quartal des Jahres 75 noch einmal 8.210 Exemplare und in den ersten zwei Monaten dieses Jahres 2.300 Exemplare verkauft, so daß wir jetzt bei einer Gesamtauflage von 263.180 stehen.

Von der Taschenbuchausgabe "Erinnerungen" wurden bis zum heutigen Tage 91.450 Exemplare verkauft. Zur Zeit steht die Taschenbuchfassung von den 1.400 Ullstein Taschenbüchern an der Spitze des Verkaufs, vor allen Unterhaltungsromanen des allgemeinen Programms.

Von der Buchausgabe der "Spandauer Tagebücher" wurden im letzten Quartal des Jahres 75 noch einmal 86.220 Exemplare und in den ersten zwei Monaten dieses Jahres 4.750 Exemplare verkauft, so daß wir jetzt bei einer Gesamtauflage von 229.070 stehen.

Mit den besten Grüßen bin ich

Wolf Jobst Siedler

Berlin, den 20. Februar 1976

83

The Speer Brand and its Inventors

84 *"... it should be avoided that (...) detrimental parts of the interview convey a negative image of Mr Speer."*

Agreement between Siedler and the responsible persons at the NDR before the interview with Speer, May 1969 (Bundesarchiv Koblenz [Federal Archive Koblenz] NL 1340/53, memo concerning the conversation on 9 May, 1969)

Speer's publisher, Wolf Jobst Siedler, marketed Speer's *Erinnerungen* [*Inside the Third Reich*] worldwide in 1969. Accompanied by major advertising and pre-prints, the book quickly became a bestseller. Joachim Fest produced a TV interview for the NDR. It was agreed with Siedler that Speer was to appear in a positive light. Joachim Fest used Speer as the central source for his Hitler biography which was published by Siedler in 1973. Together, in 1975, they produced the *Spandauer Tagebücher* [*Spandau: The Secret Diaries*]. For the pre-print in the daily newspaper *Die Welt* alone, Speer received 600,000 DM. Worldwide, around 3 million copies of the *Erinnerungen* were sold, and today around a thousand copies per year still sell.

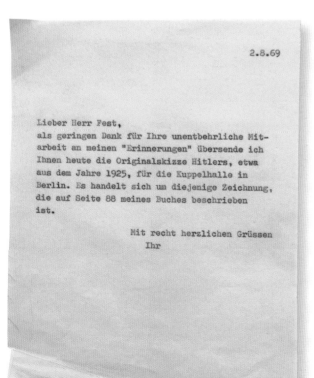

Speer's accompanying letter for the present of a sketch by Hitler to Joachim Fest, 2 August, 1969 (carbon copy) (Bundesarchiv Koblenz [Federal Archive Koblenz] NL 1340/17)

Albert Speer's Image in the USA

American publishers, Macmillan, purchased the foreign rights to the *Erinnerungen* for a minimum fee of 250,000 Dollars. For American readers, specific passages concerning Speer's supposed distancing from anti-Semitism were added. Siedler paid American journalists to promote Speer's image and his own image as publisher. The success of *Erinnerungen* and *Spandauer Tagebücher* repeated itself in the USA. In 1982, a film based on *Erinnerungen* was made for television.

Amongst the American public, Speer established for himself the image of the "good Nazi". Speer's supporters, such as Simon Wiesenthal, promoted this perception in lectures throughout the United States. Speer's relationship with Gerald Gross who marketed Speer's books in the USA was almost a friendship. In spite of his public announcements, Speer did not donate his entire American fees, but only part of them.

Albert and Margarete Speer with American publisher, Gerald Gross, 1970s
(Gerald Gross estate, private collection)

References

86   Dietmar Arnold:
> Neue Reichskanzlei und „Führerbunker". Legenden und Wirklichkeit [New Reich Chancellery and "Führer" Bunker. Legends and Reality], Berlin 2005.

Willi A. Boelcke (ed.):
> Deutschlands Rüstung im Zweiten Weltkrieg. Hitlers Konferenzen mit Albert Speer 1942–1945 [Germany's Armament Industry during World War II. Hitler's conferences with Albert Speer 1942–1945], Frankfurt am Main 1969.

Magnus Brechtken:
> „Ein Kriminalroman könnte nicht spannender erfunden werden". Albert Speer und die Historiker ["No detective story could be invented more exciting". Albert Speer and the historians], in Magnus Brechtken (ed.): Life Writing and Political Memoir – Lebenszeugnisse und politische Memoiren, Göttingen 2012, pp. 35–78.

Magnus Brechtken:
> Speer – eine deutsche Karriere [Speer – A German Career], Berlin 2017.

Heinrich Breloer:
> Die Akte Speer. Spuren eines Kriegsverbrechers [The Speer File. Traces of a War Criminal], Berlin 2005.

Heinrich Breloer:
> Speer und Er. Hitlers Architekt und Rüstungsminister [Speer and He. Hitler's Architect and Armament Minister] Berlin 2005.

Heinrich Breloer:
> Unterwegs zur Familie Speer. Begegnungen, Gespräche und Interviews [En Route to the Speer Family. Encounters, Conversations and Interviews], Berlin 2005.

André Deschan:
> Im Schatten von Albert Speer. Der Architekt Rudolf Wolters [In the Shadow of Albert Speer. The Architect Rudolf Wolters], Berlin 2016.

Werner Durth:
> Deutsche Architekten. Biographische Verflechtungen 1900–1970 [German Architects. Biographical Entanglements 1900–1970], Munich 1992.

Jörn Düwel/Niels Gutschow:
> Baukunst und Nationalsozialismus. Demonstration von Macht in Europa 1940–1943 [Art of Building and National Socialism. Demonstration of Power in Europe 1940–1943], Berlin 2015.

Joachim C. Fest:
> The Face of the Third Reich. Portraits of the Nazi Leadership, London, New York 2011.

Joachim C. Fest:
> Speer. The Final Verdict, New York 2002.

Joachim C. Fest:
> Albert Speer. Conversations with Hitler's Architect Cambridge, Malden, 2007.

Florian Freund/Bertrand Perz/Karl Stuhlpfarrer:
> Der Bau des Vernichtungslagers Auschwitz-Birkenau. Die Aktenmappen der Zentralbauleitung Auschwitz „Vorhaben: Kriegsgefangenenlager Auschwitz (Durchführung der Sonderbehandlung)" im Militärhistorischen Archiv Prag [The Construction of the Auschwitz-Birkenau Extermination Camp. The files of the Auschwitz Central Building Authority "Project Auschwitz POW Camp (Execution of Special Treatment)" in the Prague Archive for Military History] in Zeitgeschichte 20 (1993), pp. 187–214.

Ian Hamsher:
> Albert Speer. Victim of Nuremberg?, London 1970.

Gregor Janssen:
> Das Ministerium Speer. Deutschlands Rüstung im Krieg [The Speer Ministry. Germany's Armament Industry During the War], Frankfurt am Main, Berlin 1978.

Martin Kitchen:
> Speer. Hitler's Architect,New Haven, London 2015.

Stefan Krebs/Werner Tschacher:
> Speer und Er. Und wir? Deutsche Geschichte in gebrochener Erinnerung [Speer and He. And We? German History in Fragmented Memory], in Geschichte in Wissenschaft und Unterricht, 3 (2007), pp. 163–173.

Léon Krier:
> Albert Speer. Architecture 1932–1942, Brussels, 1985.

Alexander Kropp:
> Die politische Bedeutung der NS-Repräsentationsarchitektur. Die Neugestaltungspläne Albert Speers für den Umbau Berlins zur „Welthauptstadt Germania" 1936–1942 [The Political Meaning of Prestigious Nazi Architecture. Albert Speer's Plans for Re-Structuring Berlin as the "World Capital Germania" 1936–1942], Neuried 2005.

Alexander Kropp:
> „Vom Generalbauinspektor genehmigt ..." Albert Speers Medienpolitik als „Generalbauinspektor für die Reichshauptstadt (GBI) zwischen 1937 und 1944 ["Authorised by the Inspector General for Building ..." Albert Speer's Media Policies as "Inspector General for Building for the Reich Capital" (GBI) between 1937 and 1944], in Verantwortungsvolle Wissenschaft: Festschrift zum Akademischen Forum zur 122. Cartellversammlung des Cartellverbandes Katholischer Studentenverbindungen, Saturday, 3 May, 2008, pp. 107–116.

Alexander Kropp:
> Architekt und Propaganda des GBI [Architect and Propaganda of the GBI] in Wolfgang Benz et al. (eds): Kunst im NS-Staat: Ideologie, Ästhetik, Protagonisten, Berlin 2015, pp. 333–345.

Lars Olof Larsson:
> Die Neugestaltung der Reichshauptstadt. Albert Speers Generalbebauungsplan für Berlin [The Re-Design of the Reich Capital. Albert Speer's Master Plan for Berin], Stuttgart 1978.

Lars Olof Larsson/Sabine Larsson:
> „Fröhliche Neugestaltung" oder die Gigantomanie von Berlin 1937–1943. Albert Speers Generalbebauungsplan im Spiegel satirischer Zeichnungen von Hans Stephan ["Merry Re-Design" or the Gigantomania of Berlin 1937–1943. Albert Speer's Master Plan Seen in Satirical Drawings by Hans Stephan], Kiel 2008.

Hans Mommsen:
> Spandauer Tagebücher. Bemerkungen zu den Aufzeichnungen Albert Speers im Internationalen Militärgefängnis 1946–1966 [Spandau Diaries. Remarks about Albert Speer's Notes Made in the International Military Prison 1946–1966], in Politische Vierteljahresschrift 17 (1976), pp. 108–114.

Winfried Nerdinger (ed.):
Architektur und Verbrechen. Die Rolle der Architekten im Nationalsozialismus [Architecture and Crime. The Role of Architects in National Socialism], Göttingen 2014.

Margret Nissen:
Sind Sie die Tochter Speer? [Are You the Speer Daughter?], Bergisch-Gladbach 2007.

Bertrand Perz:
Verwaltete Gewalt. Der Tätigkeitsbericht des Verwaltungsführers im Konzentrationslager Mauthausen 1941 bis 1944 [Administered Violence. The Activity Report of the Head of Administration in Mauthausen Concentration Camp 1941 to 1944], Vienna 2013.

Hans-Joachim Reichhardt/Wolfgang Schäche:
Von Berlin nach Germania [From Berlin to Germania] Berlin 1984.

Adelbert Reif (ed.):
Albert Speer. Kontroversen um ein deutsches Phänomen [Albert Speer. Controversies around a German Phenomenon], Munich 1978.

Baijayanti Roy:
The Making of a Gentleman Nazi. Albert Speer's Politics of History in the Federal Republic of Germany, Frankfurt am Main 2016.

Jonas Scherner/Jochen Streb:
Das Ende eines Mythos? Albert Speer und das so genannte Rüstungswunder [The End of a Myth? Albert Speer and the So-called Armament Miracle], in Vierteljahrschrift für Sozial- und Wirtschaftsgeschichte 93,2 (2006), pp. 172–196.

Jörg Michael Schiefer/Albert Speer:
Architekt, Generalbauinspektor und Rüstungsminister. Gespräche mit Albert Speer 1971–1974 [Architect, Inspector General of Building and Armament Minister. Conversations with Albert Speer 1971–1975], Göttingen 2013.

Ulrich Schlie:
Albert Speer: „Alles, was ich weiß". Aus unbekannten Geheimdienstprotokollen vom Sommer 1945 [Albert Speer: "Everything I know". From unknown secret service minutes of summer 1945], Munich 1999.

Ulrich Schlie:
Albert Speer: Die Kransberg-Protokolle 1945. Seine ersten Aussagen und Aufzeichnungen (Juni–September) [Albert Speer: The Kransberg Minutes 1945. His first testimonies and notes (June–September)], Munich 2003.

Matthias Schmidt:
Albert Speer: Das Ende eines Mythos [Albert Speer: The End of a Myth], Berne, Munich 1982.

Angela Schönberger:
Die neue Reichskanzlei von Albert Speer. Zum Zusammenhang von nationalsozialistischer Ideologie und Architektur [Albert Speer's New Reich Chancellery. On the Link between National Socialist Ideology and Architecture], Berlin 1981.

Heinrich Schwendemann:
"Drastic Measures to Defend the Reich at the Oder and the Rhine ..." A Forgotten Memorandum of Albert Speer of 18 March 1945, in Journal of Contemporary History 38,4 (2003), pp. 597–614.

Heinrich Schwendemann:
Der „entgrenzte" Architekt. Zur Rolle Albert Speers im „Dritten Reich" [The "Unleashed" Architect. On Albert Speer's Role During the "Third Reich"], in Susanne Kuß (ed.) Der Zweite Weltkrieg in Europa und Asien. Grenzen, Grenzräume, Grenzüberschreitungen. [Professor Dr. Bernd Martin zum 65. Geburtstag), Freiburg im Breisgau 2006, pp. 33–51.

Heinrich Schwendemann:
„Verbrannte Erde"? Hitlers Nero-Befehl vom 19. März 1945 ["Scorched Earth"? Hitler's Nero Order of 19 March, 1945], in Ulrich Herbert et al. (ed.): Kriegsende in Deutschland, Hamburg 2005, pp. 158–167.

Heinrich Schwendemann:
Zwischen Abscheu und Faszination: Joachim C. Fests Hitlerbiographie als populäre Vergangenheitsbewältigung [Between Disgust and Fascination: Joachim C. Fest's Hitler Biography as a Popular Way of Dealing with the Past], in Jürgen Danyel (ed.): 50 Klassiker der Zeitgeschichte, Göttingen 2007, pp. 127–131.

Gitta Sereny:
Albert Speer. His Battle with the Truth, New York, 1995.

Sebastian Tesch:
Albert Speer (1905–1981), Vienna, Cologne, Weimar 2016.

Dagmar Thorau/Gernot Schaulinski (eds):
Mythos Germania. Vision und Verbrechen [The Germania Myth. Vision and Crime], Berlin 2014.

Isabell Trommer:
Rechtfertigung und Entlastung. Albert Speer in der Bundesrepublik [Justification and Exoneration. Albert Speer in the Federal Republic], Frankfurt, New York 2016.

Dan van der Vat:
The Good Nazi. The Life and Lies of Albert Speer, London, 1998.

Esther Vilar:
Speer, Berlin 1998.

Jens-Christian Wagner:
Produktion des Todes. Das KZ Mittelbau-Dora [Production of Death. Mittelbau-Dora Concentration Camp], Göttingen 2001.

Susanne Willems:
Der entsiedelte Jude. Albert Speers Wohnungsmarktpolitik für den Berliner Hauptstadtbau [Expulsed Jewry. Albert Speer's Housing Market Policy for the Construction of the Capital Berlin], Berlin 2015.

Susanne Willems/Frank Schumann/Fritz Schumann: Auschwitz. Die Geschichte des Vernichtungslagers [Auschwitz. The History of the Extermination Camp], Berlin 2015.

Karl-Günter Zelle:
Hitlers zweifelnde Elite. Goebbels – Göring – Himmler – Speer [Hitler's Doubting Elite. Goebbels – Göring – Himmler – Speer], Paderborn 2010.

Publisher's Imprint

Exhibition Information

88 **Albert Speer in the Federal Republic – Dealing with the German Past**

Special Exhibition of the Documentation Centre Party Rally Grounds
27 April to 26 November, 2017, Large Exhibition Hall

Exhibition Team:
Dr Martina Christmeier, Florian Dierl, Hanne Leßau,
Dr Alexander Schmidt
(Documentation Centre Party Rally Grounds, Nuremberg)

Project Leaders:
Dr Martina Christmeier, Dr Alexander Schmidt
(Documentation Centre Party Rally Grounds, Nuremberg)

Co-operation and Academic Advisor:
Prof. Dr Magnus Brechtken
(Institute for Contemporary History, Munich-Berlin)

Project Assistant:
Susanne Wagner
(undergraduate assistant, University of Bamberg)

Administrator:
Jürgen deHasque
(Documentation Centre Party Rally Grounds, Nuremberg)

PR:
Dr Martina Christmeier
(Documentation Centre Party Rally Grounds, Nuremberg)
Alexandra Foghammar
(City of Nuremberg Press and Information Office)
Tanja Heider
(Nuremberg Municipal Museums)

Experts in the Exhibition:
Prof. Dr Magnus Brechtken, Munich
Dr Heinrich Breloer, Cologne
Prof. Dr Jörn Düwel, Hamburg
Prof. Dr Bertrand Perz, Vienna
Dr Matthias Schmidt, Berlin
Dr Heinrich Schwendemann, Freiburg
Dr Isabell Trommer, Berlin
Dr Jens-Christian Wagner, Celle
Dr Susanne Willems, Berlin

Exhibition Design:
Architecture: Rainer Lendler
(Lendler Exhibition Architects, Berlin)
Graphic Design: Robert Beckand
(Studio Robert Beckand, Berlin)

Media Productions:
Jens Wunderling, Patrick Kochlik
(SYNTOP Digital Media Design, Berlin)

Film Recording and Editing:
Winfried Schuhmann, Günther Wittmann,
Christian Klonek, Kurt Keerl
(Medienwerkstatt Franken, Nuremberg)
Tobias Lindner (Kamera Interviews Berlin)

Exhibition Set-up and Electrical Installations:
Helmut Ottmann, Panagiotis Georgakopoulos
(Documentation Centre Party Rally Grounds, Nuremberg)

Exhibition Furnishings:
Annette Schubert
(Handbuch – Atelier für Papiergestaltung, Nuremberg)

Carpenter Works:
Schreinerei Lämmermann (Hersbruck)
Barthelmess, BDD Produktion GmbH (Fürth)

Printing of Exhibition Panels:
Barthelmess, BDD Produktion GmbH (Fürth)

We would like to thank the archives, agencies, television stations, institutes and private individuals for providing documents, photographs and media for the exhibition and for the catalogue, as well as numerous people who donated books for the central exhibition installation.

Catalogue Information

Editors:
Dr Martina Christmeier, Dr Alexander Schmidt
(Documentation Centre Party Rally Grounds, Nuremberg)

Concept and Editorial Team:
Dr Martina Christmeier, Dr Alexander Schmidt
(Documentation Centre Party Rally Grounds, Nuremberg)

Project Assistant:
Susanne Wagner
(undergraduate assistant, University of Bamberg)

Texts:
Prof. Dr Magnus Brechtken: pp. 4–5 and 82–85
Dr Martina Christmeier: pp. 6–7, 10–15, 45–55, 58–59, 76–81
Florian Dierl: pp. 37–43
Rainer Lendler: p. 9
Hanne Leßau: pp. 24–35, 70–73
Dr Alexander Schmidt: pp. 6–7, 10, 17–23, 57, 60–69, 74–75
Susanne Wagner: p. 86–87

Translation:
Ulrike Seeberger and Jane Britten

Graphic Design:
Martin Küchle
(Martin Küchle Kommunikationsdesign, Nuremberg)

Printing:
L/M/B Druck GmbH Louko, Nuremberg

ISBN:
978-3-7319-0594-3

Michael Imhof Verlag Gmbh & Co KG
Stettiner Straße 25, 36100 Petersberg
www.imhof-verlag.de

Despite intensive research, it was not possible in all cases to identify copyright holders for all illustrations. Where appropriate, the editorial team would be grateful for appropriate information.

We would like to thank the Mercator Foundation for its generous financial support for the catalogue.

ISBN 978-3-7319-0594-3 9,80 Euro

MICHAEL IMHOF VERLAG